IAN LIVINGSTONE

FIGHTING FANTASY

Jerome

Fighting Fantasy: new Wizard editions

1. The Warlock of Firetop Mountain
2. The Citadel of Chaos
3. Deathtrap Dungeon
4. Stormslayer
5. Creature of Havoc
6. City of Thieves
7. Bloodbones
8. Night of the Necromancer
9. House of Hell
10. Eye of the Dragon

Also available in the original Wizard editions

6. Crypt of the Sorcerer
8. Forest of Doom
9. Sorcery! 1: The Shamutanti Hills
10. Caverns of the Snow Witch
11. Sorcery! 2: Kharé – Cityport of Traps
12. Trial of Champions
13. Sorcery! 3: The Seven Serpents
14. Armies of Death
15. Sorcery! 4: The Crown of Kings
16. Return to Firetop Mountain
17. Island of the Lizard King
18. Appointment with F.E.A.R.
19. Temple of Terror
20. Legend of Zagor
22. Starship Traveller
23. Freeway Fighter
24. Talisman of Death
25. Sword of the Samurai
27. Curse of the Mummy
28. Spellbreaker
29. Howl of the Werewolf

IAN LIVINGSTONE

EYE OF THE DRAGON

Illustrated by Martin McKenna

Wizard Books

Published in the UK in 2010 by Wizard Books,
an imprint of Icon Books Ltd., Omnibus Business Centre
39–41 North Road, London N7 9DP
email: info@iconbooks.co.uk
www.iconbooks.co.uk/wizard

Previously published by Wizard Books in 2005

Sold in the UK, Europe, South Africa and Asia
by Faber & Faber Ltd., Bloomsbury House
74–77 Great Russell Street, London WC1B 3DA or their agents

Distributed in the UK, Europe, South Africa and Asia
by TBS Ltd., TBS Distribution Centre, Colchester Road,
Frating Green, Colchester CO7 7DW

Published in Australia in 2010 by Allen & Unwin Pty. Ltd.,
PO Box 8500, 83 Alexander Street, Crows Nest, NSW 2065

Distributed in Canada by Penguin Books Canada,
90 Eglington Avenue East, Suite 700, Toronto,
Ontario M4P 2Y3

ISBN: 978-1-84831-123-7

Printed and bound in the UK by
Clays of Bungay

To the Warlocks of Kilimanjaro:
Andy, Charles, Darren, Dave, Doron,
Graeme, Harry, Jeff, John, Kelly,
Mark, Roger, Sean and Tony.
Special mountain, special guys,
special memories

CONTENTS

HOW WILL YOU START
YOUR ADVENTURE?

The book you hold in your hands is a gateway to another world – a world of dark magic, terrifying monsters, brooding castles, treacherous dungeons and untold danger, where a noble few defend against the myriad schemes of the forces of evil. Welcome to the world of **Fighting Fantasy**!

You are about to embark upon a thrilling fantasy adventure in which **YOU** are the hero! **YOU** decide which route to take, which dangers to risk and which creatures to fight. But be warned – it will also be **YOU** who has to live or die by the consequences of your actions.

Take heed, for success is by no means certain, and you may well fail in your mission on your first attempt. But have no fear, for with experience, skill and luck, each new attempt should bring you a step closer to your ultimate goal.

Prepare yourself, for when you turn the page you will enter an exciting, perilous **Fighting Fantasy** adventure where every choice is yours to make, an adventure in which **YOU ARE THE HERO!**

How would you like to begin your adventure?

If you are new to Fighting Fantasy ...
You probably want to start playing straightaway. Just turn over to the next page and start reading. You may not get very far first time but you'll get the hang of how Fighting Fantasy gamebooks work.

If you have played Fighting Fantasy before ...
You'll realise that to have any chance of success, you will need to discover your hero's attributes. You can create your own character by following the instructions on pages 213–214, or, to get going quickly, you may choose one of the existing Fighting Fantasy adventurers described on pages 210–212. Don't forget to enter your character's details on the *Adventure Sheet* which appears on pages 220–221.

Game Rules
It's a good idea to read through the rules which appear on pages 213–219 before you start. But as long as you have a character on your *Adventure Sheet*, you can get going without reading the Rules – just refer to them as you need to.

BACKGROUND

Like any seasoned adventurer, you are always interested to hear rumours about gold, diamonds and hidden treasure. Unfortunately, you have been down on your luck recently and you are struggling to earn the few copper pieces needed for food and lodgings. You are hoping that your luck will soon change.

Two days ago you arrived in Fang, a town notorious for its deadly labyrinth, Deathtrap Dungeon. The annual challenge is taking place next month and the town is buzzing with excitement.

You are staying in the damp attic of the Blue Pig Tavern, sharing your room with other travellers and wretches who have fallen on hard times and so you always sleep with your sword under your pillow. One night a stranger enters the room and slumps down on the bed opposite you. Lit by the pale moonlight coming through the single window, you see that he is a tall, thick-set man dressed in dark robes that hide all but his eyes. The amount of dirt and dust on his clothes shows that he has travelled far.

You are intrigued by this stranger and offer him a drink from your flask which he accepts with a grunt. He introduces himself as Henry Delacor and he tells you of his recent adventures; how he almost lost his life in search of a legendary item of treasure.

Naturally, you are excited to hear about the treasure and offer him another drink in the hope of gaining more information. He goes on to tell you of his five-year search for a metre-high solid gold dragon with jewelled eyes. He describes in detail how he finally found the underground labyrinth that led to the golden dragon.

He tells you of all the monsters he killed in the labyrinth to reach that dragon, and how he even entered the room in which it had been hidden for years. He smiles as he recalls the pleasure of first sighting the dragon, but tells of how angry he became when he noticed that the jewelled eyes were missing. He had been told that without the eyes the dragon could not be touched as to do so would mean instant death. He was not sure if this was true or not, but he did not dare find out for himself. He left the room without touching the dragon, and began to search the labyrinth in the hope of finding the two emerald eyes.

The search almost cost him his life when he entered a cave and was attacked by a two-headed troll some three metres tall. Having survived the battle he decided to give up his quest as gold was of no use to a dead man!

You tell him that you are an adventurer, like himself, and that you would dearly like to finish his quest. You ask him to tell you where the labyrinth is located. He replies that he will on the condition that if you find the gold dragon you will bring it back to him and share the spoils from its sale.

'I promise you it is worth more than all the gold in Deathtrap Dungeon, so there will be plenty of wealth for both of us,' he says convincingly. 'At a guess I would say it's worth 335,000 gold pieces!'

You assure him that if you succeed, you will definitely return.

'In that case you won't mind drinking this!' he says gleefully while handing you a small glass bottle of purple liquid.

On asking him what it is, he tells you that it is a slow-acting poison and unless you return to him for the antidote within fourteen days you will die. You snatch the bottle from him, stare at him coldly, and drink the liquid in one gulp. He then produces a map that shows the way through Darkwood Forest to a woodcutter's hut. Inside there are stairs leading down from a trapdoor to an underground labyrinth. At that point the map ends, although he warns you that the passageways are inhabited by violent, evil people and fearsome creatures. He then lies down on his bed and goes to sleep exhausted. You try to sleep yourself but are restless and can think only about the dangerous adventure that awaits you. In the morning the mysterious stranger hands you a small leather pouch. Inside you find a large emerald cut in the shape of an eye!

'I found one. I hope you find the other. Here, take it. You will fail without it. I will wait for you here. Remember two things. One, you have fourteen days to return and no more. Two, find the matching emerald to the one I gave you and place both in the eye sockets before you touch the dragon itself,' he says very seriously.

Before setting off for Darkwood Forest, you fill your backpack with provisions, put the leather pouch and 10 Gold Pieces in your pocket and say goodbye to Henry Delacor. 'Good luck,' he says, 'you'll need it.' Then the huge, balding man extends his hand and doesn't so much shake yours as crush it. His icy blue eyes stare out from his chubby face, watching you carefully. Although he is smiling, there is something in his eyes that makes you feel uncomfortable and unwilling to trust him. But it's too late now! You set off and look back once to see him leaning against the doorway of the Blue Pig Tavern. Is there a golden dragon? Are you being slowly poisoned? What is it about Henry Delacor that makes you feel so ill at ease? No doubt all these questions will be answered in the coming days.

Now turn over.

1

The three-day trek across the Pagan Plains to Dark-wood Forest is exhausting. It passes without incident apart from an attack by two wild dogs that you quickly dispatch with your sword. The most memorable sight of the journey is the view to the east of Firetop Mountain with its distinctive red peak rising sharply up to the sky. You pass by the dwarf village of Stonebridge, cross Red River and finally enter Darkwood Forest. You follow the map through the foreboding forest and finally arrive at the wood-cutter's hut nearly five days after leaving Henry Delacor at the Blue Pig Tavern in Fang. Despite feeling tired and hungry, seeing the woodcutter's hut is a real boost to your spirits. The small hut is made of oak and its front door is open. You poke your head through the doorway and shout 'hello' in the hope of seeing the woodcutter, but the piles of dirt and debris on the floor tell you he is long gone. In the far corner of the hut you see a wood-burning stove and underneath a dirty rug you discover a trapdoor. You lift it up and see wooden steps leading down into the gloom below. If you want to search the hut first, turn to **311**. If you want to go straight down the steps, turn to **69**.

2

Confident that you have made the right choice, you step forward to pull the dagger from the wall. Turn to **280**.

3

The breastplate fits perfectly but it is not what it appears. It was made by an evil sorcerer who cursed the metal which it was made from. Even though you think the breastplate will defend you, the curse has actually weakened you. Lose 1 SKILL point, 1 LUCK point and 3 STAMINA points. Turn to **151**.

4

You cross the cavern and see that here, too, the wall is solid rock with no way out. There is a rope hanging down from the high ceiling but you cannot see where it leads to. If you want to climb up the rope, turn to **406**. If you would rather walk around the wall of the cavern in the hope of finding a way out, turn to **40**.

5

The moment you sit down in the chair you fall into a long deep sleep. You wake up hours later to find that you have been robbed. All the gold has been removed from your backpack by the Dark Elves who made the magic sleeping chair. Then you notice that your sword has also been stolen and has been replaced by a blunt, short sword. Reduce your SKILL by 2 points. But at least the Elves did not find the leather pouch containing the emerald. Angry at yourself for falling into the trap, you stride on up the corridor cursing loudly. Turn to **220**.

6

You enter a small room which is completely empty except for a playing card lying on the floor. It is the Queen of Spades and it looks slightly unusual in that the queen has a very wide grin on her face. If you want to pick up the card, turn to **129**. If you would rather leave the room and walk on, turn to **112**.

7

As the walls close in, you just have time to grab the emerald and dive through the hole in the wall. You land heavily on the floor of an enormous cave. Water drops noisily on to the floor from the tips of stalactites hanging down from the high rock ceiling. The cave is lit by a strange fluorescent fungus, which grows in patches all over the walls and gives off an eerie amber light. 'Well, is it the one we are looking for?' Littlebig asks excitedly, his words echoing loudly throughout the cave. You can hardly contain your own excitement as you untie the leather pouch given to you by Henry Delacor so you can compare the emeralds. You hold them next to each other and examine them carefully. They match! 'Yippee!' shouts Littlebig happily running around in a circle waving his hands in the air. You place both emeralds back in the pouch and tell Littlebig to calm down and look for a way out of the cave. Turn to **266**.

8

You climb slowly up the rope and peek through the hole in the ceiling. You find yourself looking inside a cluttered room that is filled with all sorts of objects: chests, armour, weapons, statues, vases, idols, sacks and boxes. It looks like a storeroom full of stolen loot. You cannot resist the urge to pull yourself up through the hole and rummage through the loot. You are almost through the tight-fitting hole when suddenly three short humanoids, just a metre tall but with large heads and mean-looking faces, jump out from behind the boxes armed with clubs. They shout at each other in high-pitched twittering voices, and one of them rushes forward to whack you on the shoulder with its club before you can free your hands to defend yourself. Lose 2 STAMINA points. You are being attacked by thieving NIBLICKS who love nothing better than to trap unwary travellers, beat them to a pulp and rob them. If you want to drop down to the corridor below and retrace your steps, turn to **144**. If you would rather fight the Niblicks, turn to **231**.

9

On the right-hand wall of the corridor you see a large oak door with big iron hinges. The skeletons of several small rodents are nailed to the door. If you wish to open the door, turn to **211**. If you wish to carry on walking up the corridor, turn to **166**.

10

You walk up to the cage and push on the door. You are amazed when it opens and the young woman immediately walks towards you. As her smile broadens you notice two long fangs extending from her upper jaw. With a crazed look of hunger on her face and her mouth wide open, the Vampire lunges at you. This undead creature is unafraid of your sword. If you have garlic, turn to **372**. If you have a silver dagger, turn to **163**. If you have neither of these, you will have to fight. Turn to **107**.

11

A deep frown appears on Littlebig's face as you raise the bottle to your lips. But you smile and wink at him and gulp down the clear liquid in one go. You feel a warm, tingling sensation as the liquid runs down your gullet. All your aches and pains from combat disappear and your scars vanish too. Gain 4 STAMINA points. You thank Pia for giving you the potion of healing.

'My pleasure,' Pia replies softly.

'I don't wish to appear rude,' Littlebig says hesitantly, 'but would you mind telling me what a nice girl like you is doing in a place like this?'

Pia raises her hand over her mouth and starts to giggle. 'Not everything is as it seems, my dear dwarf,' she replies. 'What you see is not what I am. It's an illusion brought on by another of my potions. In reality I am a lady long of age and short of teeth.' Pia then tells you that she has spent her whole life perfecting her potions, many of which are unknown in the rest of Allansia. She came to live in this dungeon to get away from people who tried to steal her secret formulas. But now and again she does sell potions to people she likes. 'Well do you like us?' Littlebig asks enthusiastically. 'So far', she replies teasingly. 'To you two I am prepared to sell my Clear Vision potion, my Water Breathing potion and my Green Skin potion. All of them cost 5 Gold Pieces each.'

After buying the potions you want, and paying Pia, you bid her farewell and leave the room. Turn to **265**.

12

The rats suddenly stop a metre in front of you, as though they have hit an invisible screen. The bracelet you are wearing, although cursed, has low level creature control magic properties. Add 1 LUCK point. The rats quickly scurry back down the hole they appeared from, making the Witch more furious than ever. She starts mumbling strange words in a low monotone voice, and you watch almost transfixed as her arms elongate from her body and transform into snakes! You have no choice but to fight the Snake Witch.

SNAKE WITCH   SKILL 10   STAMINA 6

With her venomous snake heads, the Witch has two attacks to your one. If you are bitten three times, turn to **352**. If you win, turn to **201**.

13

Floresto smiles and looks very confident as he raises his sword to signal the start of the duel.

MASTER SWORDSMAN SKILL 11   STAMINA 6

If you win, turn to 152.

14

The silver key turns the lock of the silver box. It clicks open and inside you find a polished stone etched with the words 'three axe'. Turn to 227.

15

You make a wish but nothing happens. This is not a wishing pool. If you want to reach into the pool to collect some of the gold coins and recover the Gold Piece you tossed in, turn to 369. If you want to walk directly to the door opposite, turn to 322.

16

The scroll is in fact a map of a section of the dungeon. It shows a passageway with two doors next to each other. One door has a green square painted on it and the other door has a blue triangle painted on it. The door with the green square is circled in ink with the words "this way" written underneath it. You show it to Littlebig who says, 'Let's not forget this, it could be important.' If you have not done so already, you may either uncork the flask (turn to 245) or take the sword (turn to 358). If you would rather leave these where they are and walk, turn to 212.

17

You begin to feel very ill as you rummage through your backpack for the bottle. You uncork it quickly and gulp down the potion. It acts immediately and in less than a minute you feel well again. Add 2 STAMINA points. Turn to **201**.

18

You examine the sword closely hoping to find a clue to convince you that you have made the right choice. Sweat breaks out on your forehead as you reach out to take the sword. Turn to **106**.

19

The doll is hollow and breaks into small pieces on the floor. Lying amid the clay shards you see a gold ring. Inscribed on the inside of the ring you see some strange runes which you don't understand. You hand the ring to Littlebig who presses it close to his nose to read the inscription. 'It says "ring of zombie control", I believe,' Littlebig says rather smugly. 'That could come in useful. Here, you better take it.' You place it on your middle finger before walking back down the corridor. Turn to **234**.

20

The corridor soon turns sharply left. Around the bend you see an alcove in the left-hand wall where water gently trickles from the mouth of a stone fountain carved in the shape of a hideous looking Hag. If you want to drink at the fountain, turn to **340**. If you would rather keep on walking up the corridor, turn to **136**.

21

You crawl into the dark recess which leads to the Giant Spider's lair. Your face brushes against a thick, sticky web which you claw at blindly with your hands. As your eyes adjust to the darkness you see some items among the debris. There is a glass ball, a broken dagger, an iron key with the number 34 stamped on it, a short stick sharpened at both ends and a leather pouch. Inside the pouch you find an exotic yellow flower that is dry and withered. It gives off a wonderful aroma and you feel immediately energetic and strong. Add 1 SKILL and 1 STAMINA point. After taking any of the items that you want, you manage to climb slowly out of the pit and carry on up the corridor. Turn to **98**.

22

The Hanging Snake is very quick to strike. You swing your sword at the incoming tail, but miss. The tail coils itself around you so that you are unable to move and barely able to breathe. Slowly, the snake rises upwards carrying you with it into its lair in the ceiling. Its enormous head and jaw will have no trouble in devouring you within the next hour. And there is nothing that Littlebig can do to help you. Your adventure is over.

23

The ugly Ogre grunts and snuffles but doesn't wake up. Sweat runs down your brow as you reach the chair. The acrid smell of the Ogre's unwashed body fills your nostrils. Slowly you lift the bag off the back of the chair and tiptoe out of the cave. In the corridor you open the bag to find a dagger and a gold ring which fits nicely on the thumb of your left hand. Breathing a sigh of relief, you walk on. Turn to **139**.

24

As you try to uncork the bottle it slips out of your hand and shatters on the stone floor. You see wisps of white smoke escaping from the broken bottle and, thinking it may be poisonous gas, you decide to run out of the cavern. Lose 1 LUCK point and turn to **76**.

25

When you lift the lid of the box the whispering voice changes to hysterical laughter. At the same time purple-coloured gas escapes from the box and envelops you completely. You start coughing uncontrollably and wherever you move the gas cloud follows. Soon you are gasping for air and start to choke. You have sprung a trap of poisonous gas and nothing can save you. Your adventure is over.

26

The door opens into a cold room which is empty except for a large mirror hanging on the wall. There is another door in the opposite wall. If you would like to look in the mirror, turn to **51**. If you would rather walk past it and open the door opposite, turn to **243**.

27

You attack the Ghost from behind as it faces Littlebig in frantic combat. But your sword simply cuts right through the Ghost, as though it wasn't there, causing it no harm at all. You yell at Littlebig to make a run for it. The Ghost turns to you as Littlebig runs for the door.

GHOST GUARDIAN   SKILL 8   STAMINA 0

If you win an Attack Round, you do not cause the Ghost any damage. It just gives you the chance to try to escape. *Test Your Luck.* If you are Lucky, turn to **401**. If you are Unlucky, turn to **263**.

28

You cannot stop yourself from falling over backwards. The Uglukk Orc seizes its opportunity and swings its mighty club into your side with a dull thud. Lose 1 SKILL point and 2 STAMINA points. If you are still alive, you roll over in great pain and try to get back on your feet before the Uglukk can strike again. Turn to **313**.

29

The cell starts to cloud with dust as you rummage through the dirt, making you cough. You find bits of old bone, fragments of rock, some huge toenail clippings which must have come from a giant creature, and some torn rags. You are about to give up the search when your fingers find a small velvet pouch. You untie the knotted string and find two items inside the pouch: a gold bracelet and a gold nugget. You put the nugget in your pocket and decide what to do with the bracelet. If you want to put it on your wrist, turn to **272**. If you would rather leave it behind and jump down into the room below, turn to **64**.

30

If you are wearing a silver armband, turn to **56**. If you are not wearing a silver armband, turn to **279**.

31

The stone clatters along the tunnel until it comes to rest somewhere out of sight. You listen carefully and hear the distant sound of a deep growl. Lose 1 LUCK point. 'Whoever or whatever is at the end of the tunnel knows we are here now!' says Littlebig somewhat apprehensively. You decide that you must crawl along the tunnel straight away and be ready for combat at any time. Turn to **405**.

32

The liquid seems to burn your throat, but the feeling changes to a soothing glow. You have drunk a potion of healing. Add 2 STAMINA points. There is a little of the potion left so you replace the cork in the bottle and put it in your backpack. Feeling a lot stronger, you leave the room and continue up the corridor. Turn to **336**.

33

Much to your relief, none of the ceiling stones hit either Littlebig or you. 'Phew!' Littlebig says exhaling noisily. 'That was a little too close for comfort'. You gasp a sigh of relief, slap him on the back and walk on. Turn to **255**.

34

The iron key turns the lock of the iron box. It clicks open and inside you find a polished stone etched with the words 'one spear'. Turn to **227**.

35

Taking one end of the heavy lid each, Littlebig and you strain to lift it. Huffing and puffing, with one mighty heave you manage to lift it a centimetre and slide it on to the floor. It lands with a crash, breaking into several large pieces. Something starts to rise out of the chest and now you realize it is not a chest but a stone coffin. An armoured skeleton with a golden crown on its skull steps out of the coffin brandishing a long sword.

SKELETON KING　　　SKILL 9　　STAMINA 7

Edged weapons like swords and daggers do little harm to Skeletons. You will only cause it to lose 1 STAMINA point during a successful Attack Round. But in each Attack Round you have two attacks to the Skeleton King's one because Littlebig can fight too. If you win, turn to **399**.

36

Littlebig sighs and says in a disgruntled voice, 'I can't believe you want to keep rummaging around in this cockroach-infested stink hole.' You decide to rip open some of the sacks. Most are filled with grain which has long since turned to dust, thanks to the mites and assorted insects that have been feeding without interruption for years. Suddenly a silver ball rolls out of one of the open sacks on to the floor. If you want to pick up the ball, turn to **256**. If you would rather agree with Littlebig and leave the room and walk on, turn to **346**.

37

Although made of old iron, the breastplate you are now wearing is magical. It seems to glow in the semi-darkness and you feel suddenly more powerful. Add 1 SKILL point and 1 LUCK point. There is nothing else of interest in the room except for some dried leaves that you find inside a brown leather pouch. The leaves give off a very unpleasant smell. After deciding whether or not to take the leaves, you leave the room and continue walking up the corridor. Turn to **151**.

38

'Try a different weapon,' says Littlebig casually. But when you try to let go you find that you can't. Your hands seem to be stuck to it like glue. Suddenly you feel a shock run up your arm like a bolt of electricity. It happens again, only with greater force. You struggle to free yourself but cannot. When you are hit a third time you pass out and are left dangling helplessly. There is nothing Littlebig can do to save you as another bolt of electricity finishes you off. Your adventure is over.

39

You empty your backpack on to the floor and pick out all the gold coins and items that you have. After repacking your other items, you walk slowly back-wards towards the door as the image of Vigdis stares at you in silence. Feeling fortunate to have escaped from the Snake Witch with your life, you hurry on up the corridor. Turn to **323**.

40

You follow the cavern wall all the way around until you arrive back at the staircase which leads up to the alcove. There doesn't appear to be any other option other than to climb it. Turn to **318**.

41

You try with all your might to raise your hands to shield your eyes but find it impossible. Lose 1 STAMINA point. As the pain increases you draw your sword and try to smash the mirror. Turn to **258**.

42

The door opens into a long room that is lined on both sides with what must be hundreds of hanging swords. At the far end of the room a man wearing leather armour is in the middle of a sword fight with a ghostly figure that is brandishing a real sword. The fighting is frantic, with the blades clashing noisily against each other. The man in the leather armour suddenly shouts out two strange words and the ghostly figure stops moving, as though frozen to the spot. The man turns to you and says, 'My name is Floresto and I am a master swordsman. Fight me if you dare and the winner takes all!' If you want to accept the challenge, turn to **13**. If you would rather refuse and walk on up the corridor, turn to **238**.

43

The Troll's axe is too big and heavy for you to use so you leave it on the floor. You rummage through the debris and find 2 Gold Pieces, a silver charm in the shape of a lion's head, a broken dagger and a silver arrow head. After putting the items you want in your backpack, you leave the room and continue up the corridor. Turn to **166**.

44

You walk along briskly and suddenly you hear the faint sound of stone grating against stone.

'Oh, oh!' Littlebig says. 'Quick! Flatten yourself against the wall.' Four square sections of the ceiling drop to the floor with a great crashing sound. *Test Your Luck*. If you are Lucky, turn to **33**. If you are Unlucky, turn to **316**.

45

In slow, jerky steps, the Skeletons advance towards you. Their mouths hang open as if they are screaming a silent battle cry. Fortunately the corridor is narrow and you can fight them one at a time.

	SKILL	STAMINA
First SKELETON	6	5
Second SKELETON	5	6

If you win, turn to **309**.

46

With strenuous effort Littlebig manages to hack off six of the spiked horns. Looking pleased with himself, he places them in his backpack before setting off to look for a way out of the cave. Turn to **199**.

47

You pick up the shovel and commence digging in the sand pit. Thirty minutes of digging yields an old wooden chest, a leather-bound book with most of its pages ripped out, a broken chair, a torn flag bearing the symbol of a wolf's head and a wooden staff. Will you:

Open the wooden chest?	Turn to **327**
Open the book?	Turn to **165**
Strike the staff on the floor?	Turn to **198**

48

The flying shards of metal shoot past you but miraculously none hit you. They miss Littlebig too. 'I told you we should have left this dump,' Littlebig says with a smirk on his face. As you leave the store room you tell him that you will take his advice next time. Turn to **346**.

49

Littlebig can hardly contain himself, such is his excitement as you take the emeralds from your leather pouch and place them in the eye sockets of the dragon. They fit perfectly. Then you and Littlebig stand on either side of the dragon and prepare to lift the heavy treasure. 'One, two, three, lift!' says Littlebig gleefully. The dragon is very heavy but you manage to lift it down from its plinth. While you are packing the dragon inside your backpack, Littlebig looks around the chamber. Finding nothing of interest, he wanders back to the plinth and sits down on it. As he does so you hear a click, and a section of the wall at the back of the chamber starts to rise up into the ceiling. Daylight floods into the chamber and it is so bright that it hurts your eyes. 'We're free!' shouts Littlebig excitedly. He strides out of the chamber and you follow him out on to a ledge that is halfway up the side of a rocky hill. A heavy-set man with a familiar face is standing on the ledge and smiles as though he was expecting you. It's Henry Delacor and you wonder what he is doing here as you had agreed to meet him back at the Blue Pig Tavern. 'Sharcle!' screams Littlebig with sudden anger. 'Why you no good, thieving coward.'

'How is it?' replies Henry Delacor, or Sharcle, or whoever he really is, still smiling that same insincere smile that you remember so well. 'How's what?' asks Littlebig.

'How's this!' he says as he pulls out a small crossbow from under his robes and fires it at Littlebig from short range. The bolt flies out and hits your friend in the chest with a dull thump. Littlebig staggers back and slumps to the floor. You run to him but he is bleeding badly.

'I should have finished him off in his cell, but maybe he helped you bring the dragon to me. How funny. Yes, I am indeed Henry Delacor but my thief friends know me as Sharcle. Now, if you would just like to hand over the dragon to me, I will happily give you the antidote you need for the poison I gave you. Now that's what I call a fair deal!' You stare back at the man with hatred in your eyes. You have never been so angry in your life. Your friend lies dying in a pool of blood. Suddenly you don't care about the antidote. All you seek is revenge. You draw your sword and step forward to attack the lying thief who drops his crossbow and draws his own sword.

SHARCLE   SKILL 8   STAMINA 8

If you win two Attack Rounds, turn to **400**.

The lid pops up quite easily and lands with a clatter on the floor. As you both lean over to take a peek inside the barrel, two bloated, hairy JUMPING SPIDERS spring out of the barrel. One lands on Littlebig's long beard and the other lands on your arm. It scurries up your arm intent on sinking its poisonous fangs in your neck. Instinctively you try to brush it off with your hand. *Test Your Luck*. If you are Lucky, turn to **118**. If you are Unlucky, turn to **392**.

51

As you look into the mirror, your body is gripped by a terrible pain. Try as you might, you find it impossible to look away. Lose 2 STAMINA points. If you want to try to cover your eyes with your hands, turn to **41**. If you would rather try to smash the mirror with your sword, turn to **258**.

52

Holding the moonstone brooch in your outstretched hand, you walk towards the evil wizard. When he catches sight of the brooch, the look on his face suddenly changes from anger to that of fear. He covers his eyes and starts to scream as though in pain. He suddenly barges past you and runs down the passageway, his screams amplified by their echoes against the stone walls. You turn to go after him but Littlebig stops you. 'Let him go. He is of no use to us,' says Littlebig. 'And besides we are on a mission and you cannot afford to be late!' Thinking back to the slow-acting poison that you drank in the Blue Pig Tavern you nod in agreement and continue on up the corridor. Turn to **291**.

53

The door opens into a room that is empty apart from twelve large portraits that line the redwood walls. There is only one portrait on the far wall, but it is much larger than the others. It depicts a bearded man standing proudly in plate armour with his sword in his right hand and his helmet tucked under his left arm. Will you:

Take a closer look at the portraits?	Turn to 373
Close the door and walk on?	Turn to 70
Go back to the door with the green square?	Turn to 141

54

The corridor soon turns sharply right and you arrive at a doorway in the left-hand wall. The door is slightly ajar and through it you can hear a woman's voice chanting a strange rhyme. If you want to open the door, turn to 254. If you would rather carry on walking up the corridor, turn to 323.

55

The pit is just too wide for you to jump over. Your fingers catch the edge on the far side, but you are unable to hang on and tumble down into the dark depths to land heavily below. Lose 3 STAMINA points. If you survive, there is no time to recover as a GIANT SPIDER scurries out of a dark recess on its long hairy legs, intent on feasting on your corpse! You are trapped and must fight.

GIANT SPIDER   SKILL 7   STAMINA 8

If you win, turn to 21.

56

You sense there is something very strange about the old man. He looks as though he is desperate to do something but is unable to do so. Little do you know that the armband used to belong to a powerful cleric who spent his time ridding the world of demons, and it is protecting you now from a terrible attack by a Lesser Demon. You ask the old man if he has any knowledge of the emerald eye but he does not reply. 'Let's keep moving,' Littlebig whispers nervously, 'I don't trust this fellow'. If you want to follow the left-hand passage, turn to **169**. If you want to follow the right-hand passage, turn to **286**. If you would rather attack the old man, turn to **160**.

57

The Witch is now angrier than ever. She starts mumbling strange words in a low monotone voice and you watch almost transfixed as her arms elongate from her body, transforming into snakes! You have no choice but to fight the hideous Snake Witch.

SNAKE WITCH   SKILL 10   STAMINA 6

With her venomous snake heads, the Witch has two attacks to your one. If you are bitten three times, turn to **352**. If you win, turn to **201**.

58

When you point the ring in their direction, the Zombies stop in their tracks. Their mouths open as if to scream, but no sound comes out. One by one they turn and shuffle off into the gloom of the cavern. When they have gone, you notice a leather pouch on the floor that must have fallen out of the pocket of one of the Zombies' tattered clothes. If you want to open the leather pouch, turn to **287**. If you want to walk on, turn to **376**.

59

The dark and musty corridor eventually splits offering you the choice to go left or right. If you wish to go left, turn to **250**. If you wish to go right, turn to **124**.

60

Breathing heavily, and soaked with perspiration, you slump down on the floor next to Littlebig. His face is still vacant-looking after his trauma, but after a drink of water and some warm words of encouragement from you, he slowly returns to his old self. 'I can't believe that creature could force me to attack you,' he says, shaking his head, 'and how did it manage to change itself into another me?' While you are listening to Littlebig, you notice another small tunnel entrance in the wall opposite. If you want to continue your quest and crawl through the new tunnel, turn to **233**. If you would rather search the cavern first, turn to **364**.

61

You are suspicious of the old man and, sensing that something is not quite right, you keep your eye on him as you turn the corner. There is an unpleasant smell of sulphur in the air and that is usually a telltale sign of evil. You trust your instinct and turn around to attack the old man. Turn to **160**.

62

The pendant you are wearing is a lucky charm. Add 1 LUCK point. It also has another magical property: it will glow brightly if somebody you are talking to is lying. Feeling pleased with your new treasure, you leave the room. Turn to **365**.

63

For each Flesh Grub that is alive you must again lose 1 STAMINA point as they strip away your skin and burrow into your arms. But Littlebig comes to your rescue and pulls the remaining grubs off you and crushes them underfoot. 'Nasty little brutes,' he says, while checking the tunic carefully for any remaining grubs. Turn to **102**.

64

The room is a disused torture chamber. An iron maiden lies open on the floor and in the far corner you see a wooden rack. Old blood-stained instruments of pain litter the ground. A strong musty smell fills the still air making you feel a little queasy. Almost hidden by a pile of chains you see an iron chest. If you want to open the chest, turn to **131**. If you would rather leave the chamber, turn to **317**.

65

You walk along the corridor and soon arrive at a T-junction. On the stone floor you see chalk arrows leading up the corridor to your right. If you want to follow the arrows, turn to **387**. If you would rather turn left, turn to **304**.

66

You react too slowly to prevent the rat from biting you. This is no ordinary rat. You have been bitten by a Fang Rat that injects strong poison into its prey like a venomous snake. Lose 1 SKILL point and 4 STAMINA points. If you are still alive, you watch the Fang Rat jump off your leg and disappear back into its hole in the wall. Littlebig grunts and says, 'Do you know what? It's just my gut feeling, but I think we are going the wrong way. I think we should go the way that person did a few minutes ago.' You decide to take Littlebig's advice and go back to the corner where the figure disappeared. Turn to **206**.

67

The fat man suddenly disappears in a puff of smoke and is replaced on the floating cushion by a small brooch made of moonstone. You pin it on to your tunic wondering what magic it holds. If you have not done so already you may search the bodies (turn to **299**) or leave the cavern (turn to **76**).

68

A thorough search of the room reveals nothing more than a bone charm on a leather cord. There are symbols etched on the charm but neither you nor Littlebig understand their meaning. If you want to put the charm around your neck, turn to **324**. Otherwise you can put it in your pocket and either let Littlebig touch the glass ball with his dagger (turn to **386**) or leave the cellars and return to the corridor above (turn to **355**).

69

The stairs lead down to a gloomy, stone-walled corridor that is lit by a few flickering torches. In the dim light you can just see that there is thick slime dripping down the walls. There is an unpleasant stench in the air. You hear a scampering noise and look down to see rats running across the muddy floor in front of you. Ahead the corridor soon splits at a junction. If you want to turn left, turn to **186**. If you want to turn right, turn to **88**.

70

A few minutes later you see a message written on the right-hand wall in large chalk letters. It reads "Go back or face certain death". 'That message is clear enough,' says Littlebig with a grin on his face. 'So what should we do?' If you want to walk on, turn to **209**. If you want to turn around and go back, you may, if you have not done so already, either open the door with the blue triangle (turn to **53**) or open the door with the green square (turn to **141**).

71

You try to look sincere and tell Vigdis that she is beautiful. Her eyes narrow to slits and she says in a cold voice, 'Not only are you a fool you are also a liar, and a cowardly one at that. I am hideously ugly and that's just the way I like it. I hate beauty. Now give me all your gold otherwise I will change you into a bat!' If you want to give Vigdis all your gold, turn to **39**. If you would rather refuse her demand, turn to **268**.

72

Holding your breath, you slide the ring slowly on to the first finger of your right hand. You wait for something terrible to happen but nothing does. If you have not done so already, you can break the glass wasp (turn to **171**) or continue walking up the passage (turn to **291**).

73

It's a long drop to the rock floor and you land heavily. Roll 1 die and reduce your STAMINA by this number. If you are still alive you may either follow the wall around the cavern (turn to **40**) or have a rest (turn to **314**).

74

You grab hold of the rope and walk back with it as far as you can. Then you run up to the edge of the pit with great speed and swing across. Turn to **190**.

75

This time as you charge Lo Lo Mai the lightning bolt that shoots from her crystal is much more powerful. It hits you like a sledgehammer and sends you crashing into the wall. As everything goes dark, you can just hear Lo Lo Mai reciting another rhyme.

> *'Proud dwarf go now as you're told*
> *Forget your pointless search for gold*
> *I tried to help you with my voice*
> *But your foolish friend left me no choice.'*

You hear Littlebig start to argue but then you lose consciousness. Your adventure is over.

76

A small alcove comes into view in the right-hand wall of the corridor. The alcove houses a magnificently carved wooden chair with the words 'Rest Ye Well' engraved in the seat. If you want to sit on the chair, turn to **5**. If you would rather carry on walking, turn to **220**.

77

Miraculously all the darts miss you and fly past to hit the walls opposite. It occurs to you that all the blood on the floor is from victims of the darts. You decide to turn around and open the door behind you (turn to **277**).

78

As you run past the Zombies, the one closest to you lashes out at you with its clawed hand. *Test your Luck.* If you are Lucky, turn to **164**. If you are Unlucky, turn to **339**.

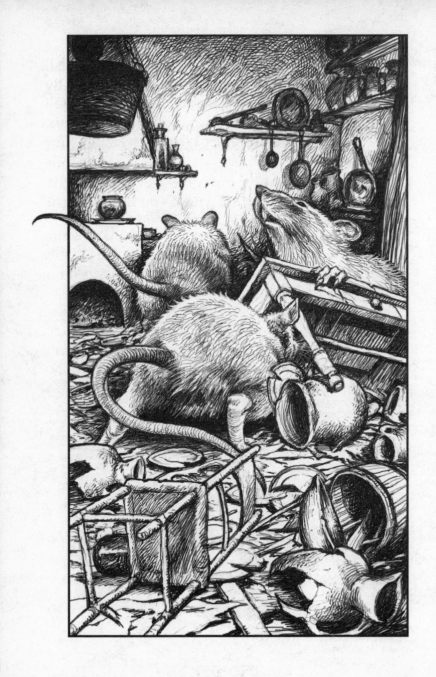

79

You enter a disused kitchen where the dirty cupboards are crammed with broken boxes, old buckets, cracked bowls and dented cooking utensils. A table with one leg missing lies upturned next to a pile of rotten potatoes. Three GIANT RATS are gnawing on some old leather boots in the far corner and do not seem to notice you. If you want to leave the kitchen before you are seen, turn to **336**. If you want to fight the Rats, you can do so one at a time.

	SKILL	STAMINA
First GIANT RAT	5	4
Second GIANT RAT	5	3
Third GIANT RAT	5	2

If you win, turn to **229**.

80

The Ogre's eyes suddenly open and it jumps up, grabbing its club. It lets out a fearsome roar and swings its club at you in anger.

OGRE   SKILL 8   STAMINA 10

If you win, turn to **319**.

81

The Wizard's blade strikes your arm causing a deep gash. It's painful but appears not to be serious. However, as you lunge forward to counter attack, you feel unbelievably weak and drop your sword. The Wizard begins to laugh. 'Ha! That will teach you to attack the mighty Malbus! Your life is draining away thanks to the evil power of my wyrm sword.' You try to move but fall head first to the ground. Your adventure is over.

82

You have drunk some very strong poison, but luckily for you it is counteracted by the magic properties of your turquoise ring. Add 1 LUCK point. The dull pain quickly disappears and you feel well again. If you have not done so already, you may either open the leather bag (turn to 114) or take the sword (turn to 358). Your only other option is to walk on, turn to 212.

83

Exhausted after the long fight, you sit down on the floor to recover. You watch on in horror as the Vampire's body crumbles into dust. A bat emerges from the dust and flies away, carrying with it the Vampire's spirit. In two days time the Vampire will return in human form and will come looking for you to exact her revenge. Suddenly you notice something else lying in the pile of dust – a jewel on a gold chain. The jewel is an emerald but, much to your disappointment, it is square and not at all shaped like a dragon's eye. You place it quickly in the black pouch in your pocket and leave the room in a great deal of excitement. Turn to **116**.

84

You tell Littlebig to calm down and remind him that you were told by Henry Delacor that both emerald eyes had to be put into their sockets before the dragon could be lifted. Littlebig hurls the dagger at the wall in anger and says, 'I can't believe we have come so far and failed. I thought we had searched every inch of this infernal dungeon. How could we have missed the emerald? Maybe your friend was wrong. Let's put one emerald in its socket and lift the dragon. I'm not going back now.' The thought of turning around and going back also fills you with dread. You take the emerald from its pouch and place it in its socket. It fits perfectly. Then, standing either side of the dragon, you and Littlebig get ready to lift it. Littlebig smiles and says, 'One, two, three, lift!' But as soon as you touch the dragon, you trigger a trap. Over thirty needle-like, poison-tipped darts shoot out of tiny holes in the plinth on which the dragon stands. Three hit you in one leg and two hit you in the other leg. Littlebig is hit by nine darts. The poison is deadly and there is no antidote. You both drop to the floor, pulling desperately at the darts. But it's no use. Although in great pain, Littlebig manages a smile and, jovial to the end, he says, 'I hear there is a lost chest filled with diamonds in the Moonstone Mines. Let's go there next…'. He never finishes his sentence and slumps over. Seconds later, so do you. Your adventure is over.

85

The bronze key turns the lock of the bronze box. It clicks open and inside you find a polished stone etched with the words 'two arrow'. Turn to **227**.

86

The scroll is ancient and brittle. You unroll it slowly as you fear it might crumble into small pieces. The once white paper is now dark amber with age and the ink writing has faded badly. In large ancient script you read the words 'Hole in the Wall'. Underneath this heading you read the secret of a magic spell that will allow you to make a hole in a wall by saying the words 'Azang Bazang-zang'. You whisper the words to yourself to remember them and as you do so the scroll crumbles into dust, its secret gone forever. But you remember the spell and one day it might save your life. Now if you have not done so already, you may pick up the black sword (turn to **345**) or examine the painting (turn to **184**). If you would rather climb back down the rope and walk back down the corridor, turn to **144**.

87

As the Verminspawn gets closer, you feel a surge of courage. You raise Skullsplitter above your head in both hands and charge at the vile beast.

VERMINSPAWN   SKILL 10   STAMINA 10

During each Attack Round, you will have two attacks, one for yourself and one for Littlebig who has a SKILL of 8. However, the Verminspawn will focus its attacks on you. If you win, turn to **380**.

88

You turn left into another similar dark corridor. This passage turns a sharp left and then continues straight on, soon arriving at a doorway in the right-hand wall. You press your ear to the large oak door and hear the sound of somebody humming. If you want to open the door, turn to **119**. If you would rather walk on, turn to **236**.

89

The soup is a thick, tasty vegetable broth that is very nourishing. You share it with Littlebig who slurps it down enthusiastically, wiping his bearded, dribbling mouth with the back of his hand before letting out a rather noisy and crude belch. 'That's good!' he says beaming. 'I wonder who made it?' Add 1 STAMINA point. If you have not done so already, you may read the sheets of paper (turn to **240**). Otherwise you can open the door opposite (turn to **312**).

90

Your strength slowly starts to drain away, but you do not know it is due to the helmet. Lose 5 STAMINA points. If you are still alive, *Test your Luck*. If you are Lucky, turn to **222**. If you are Unlucky, turn to **385**.

91

You sense something strange about the old man and watch him carefully as you turn the corner to walk past him. Although you did not know it, the armband used to belong to a powerful cleric who spent his time ridding the world of demons. Had the armband not protected you, the little old man might not have been so harmless as he appeared. You hurry on until the old man is out of sight. Turn to **169**.

92

With your sword in hand, you run down the corridor and turn the corner. A short distance ahead, the corridor ends at a T-junction where you see the person turn right and disappear again. As you approach the junction you see a white symbol on the wall ahead. Turn to **308**.

93

There is nothing you can do to stop the blade piercing your throat. You sink to your knees slowly as the blood pours from the deep wound. Your adventure is over.

94

During all the commotion in the last room, you didn't notice that a small hole was made in your backpack by Floresto's sword. You also did not realize that something fell out. Lose 1 item from your *Adventure Sheet*. Oblivious to the loss, you walk on. Turn to **238**.

95

As you start to speak, you hear the noise of fluttering wings above you. Looking up, you just have time to draw your sword to defend yourself against the two large VAMPIRE BATS that are swooping down to attack you. Fight them one at a time.

	SKILL	STAMINA
First VAMPIRE BAT	5	4
Second VAMPIRE BAT	5	4

While you are fighting the first Vampire Bat, the second will cling to your neck to suck your blood. You must lose 1 STAMINA point per Attack Round until you are able to fight it. If you win, turn to **241**.

96

The Evil Wizard stops muttering when he sees the pile of Gold Pieces cupped in your hands. He raises one of his eyebrows and looks at you suspiciously. 'I don't like this,' Littlebig whispers nervously. Suddenly the Evil Wizard bursts out laughing and says, 'Ah, a peace offering from a grovelling little toad. Thank you, I'll take your gold. Now here's my gift to you!' He raises his arms and mutters a spell to release another fireball at you from point blank range. Reduce your total of Gold Pieces to zero and roll two dice. If the number rolled is less than or equal to your SKILL score, turn to **267**. If the number rolled is greater than your SKILL, turn to **216**.

97

Convinced that the dwarf you are about to fight is not Littlebig but a Doppelgänger imitating him, you wield your sword in a frenzied attack. Suddenly the dwarf starts to metamorphose into a hideous creature some two metres tall with large scarlet scales covering its massive chest and an oversized, pulsating skull. Its eyes are large and red-veined, and its mouth is small but crammed with long needle-like fangs. There is no doubting who the DOPPELGÄNGER is now.

DOPPELGÄNGER   SKILL 10   STAMINA 10

During each Attack Round you must reduce your SKILL by 2 as you must use all your mental strength to fight the mental powers of the creature. Meanwhile, Littlebig manages to break free from the Doppelgänger's mind control but is too exhausted and drained to help you in combat. If you win, turn to **60**.

98

You continue along the dimly lit corridor until you come to another doorway in the left-hand wall. The door is unlocked. If you want to open the door, turn to **167**. If you want to carry on without further delay, turn to **151**.

99

Running along after the hooded figure, you do not see two more dark-robed figures hiding in the shadows of a small alcove. As you run past them, one thrusts a wooden staff at your legs, tripping you and sending you crashing to the floor. In an instant they are on top of you, punching and kicking as hard as they can. Lose 1 STAMINA point. You manage to free an arm to land a few blows yourself and stand up to fight the THIEVES one at a time.

	SKILL	STAMINA
First THIEF	6	6
Second THIEF	7	5

If you win, turn to 382.

100

You tell Vigdis that she is disgustingly ugly. She smiles and says, 'Thank you. Nobody has paid me such a compliment in years. You are obviously a person of great taste. You are free to go. And please take the wooden box from the shelf in the corner of the room, as a token of my appreciation.' As you leave the room, you take a peek inside the box and find a few garlic cloves, 7 Gold Pieces, a large tooth and a bronze key with the number 85 stamped on it. You pack the items away and carry on up the corridor. Turn to 323.

101

As you put your hand slowly into the hole, Littlebig shakes his head and tells you that you must be mad. You half expect to feel terrible pain as some unseen creature bites your hand off, but nothing happens. You reach further into the hole until your shoulder is pressed hard against the wall and your fingertips touch something that feels soft. Your immediate thought is that it is a rat and you withdraw your arm quickly. But convincing yourself that it is not a rat you reach back into the hole and pull out what turns out to be an old sock! Inside the sock you find 3 Gold Pieces, a small silver cross and a wavy-bladed knife. 'Some people have all the luck!' Littlebig says shaking his head. 'That's no ordinary knife, that's a kris knife. They are made by the demon priests of the abyss. Their blades are forged in cursed flames and are the only blades that can pierce the skin of a Lesser Demon.' You place the unholy knife in your belt, pocket the other findings and walk on. Turn to **354**.

102

Satisfied that there are no more grubs hidden in the warrior's tunic, you decide what to do. Will you:

Open the leather bag?	Turn to **114**
Uncork the silver flask?	Turn to **245**
Take the sword?	Turn to **358**
Leave everything and walk on?	Turn to **212**

103

The laughter gets louder and louder but you cannot tell where it is coming from as it echoes around the room. It turns into a piercing shriek which is painful to your ears. You begin to lose your sense of balance and fall over feeling violently ill. The door through which you entered the room slams shut, trapping you inside. Using all your energy, you just manage to crawl over to the footmarks and haul yourself up to stand on them. There is a sudden blinding flash and it seems as though the room is spinning. You are unable to stop yourself from passing out. Turn to **215**.

104

You both heave on the door with all your might. It opens slowly, with its hinges squeaking noisily in protest. You find yourself in a cold, dark room that has a marble plinth in the middle. On top of the plinth is a large ball made of green glass. Littlebig walks up to it but you warn him against touching it in case it's a trap. 'I think there is something inside the glass ball,' he says, peering closely at it. 'I'm just going to touch it with my dagger.' Will you:

Let Littlebig touch the glass ball?	Turn to **386**
Leave the cellars and return to the corridor above?	Turn to **355**
Look for something else in the room?	Turn to **68**

105

Scratched, bruised and battered, you land with a thump at the bottom of a dark pit. There is no time to recover as a GIANT SPIDER scurries out of a dark recess on its long hairy legs, intent on feasting on your corpse. You are trapped and must fight.

GIANT SPIDER   SKILL 7   STAMINA 8

If you win, turn to **21**.

106

With nervous anticipation you take hold of the sword in both hands and begin to pull. It does not move, so you put one leg up against the wall and pull harder. Turn to **38**.

107

The Vampire sneers at you contemptuously as you swing your sword at her. Normal weapons are almost ineffective against the undead! But there is no alternative now but to fight.

VAMPIRE   SKILL 10   STAMINA 12

If you defeat the Vampire, turn to **83**. If you wish to try to *Escape*, which you may only do after 6 Attack Rounds, you will have to *Test your Luck*. If you are Lucky, you may *Escape* through the door, turn to **116**. If you are Unlucky, you must fight on to the death.

108

There is a new passageway in the left-hand wall that you see some fifty metres ahead. A hooded figure wearing dark robes suddenly appears from around the corner carrying a black sack over his shoulder. In his right hand you see a long dagger. The figure catches sight of you, stops in his tracks, turns and runs back from where he came. 'Hey! Come back!' Littlebig shouts. His cries echo down the corridor but the hooded figure does not return. You decide to give chase and turn left down the new corridor. Turn to **224**.

109

'That's very interesting,' says the wizard after hearing your tale. 'I admire your spirit and I'm going to help you. Here is a little gift for you. Good luck.' There is a sudden flash of light and a wooden box appears in the centre of the room. Inside the box you find a gold key with the number 325 stamped on the barrel. You place it in your pocket and leave the room. Turn to **65**.

110

After Lo Lo Mai has been paid her 10 Gold Pieces, she walks over to the door and opens it for you, gesturing for you to walk through it. In the circumstances, you think that this offer is the best you can hope for. Turn to **396**.

111

As you open the door, a horrible stench fills your nostrils. You enter a large, dirty cavern, the floor of which is covered with rotten food, old bones, insects and leaking buckets of foul green liquid. Sitting at a roughly-made wooden table are two ugly brutes with warty brown-green skin. They look disgusting and smell like they have never washed in their lives. They are grunting and slavering as they stuff their large fanged mouths with what looks like intestines and rats' heads. There is no doubt about it, they are ORCS. But these are not ordinary Orcs. These two are tall, powerful and extremely violent Uglukk Orcs. They turn to look at you and belch in contempt. Black greasy drool runs down their chins, which they wipe with the back of their enormous hands. Pushing the table away, one of them rises slowly and reaches for its large morning star. The other grabs its heavy club but stays seated to watch the fight. The first Orc lets out a deafening roar and strides towards you. This will be a fearsome fight to the death.

UGLUKK ORC   SKILL 8   STAMINA 8

If you win, turn to **285**.

112

Further up the passageway you see another door on the right-hand wall. You listen at the door and hear scratching sounds coming from the other side. If you want to enter the room, turn to **79**. If you wish to carry on walking up the passageway, turn to **336**.

113

You find a velvet bag concealed inside the Evil Wizard's robes. Inside the bag you find 5 Gold Pieces, a gold ring with a large turquoise stone set in it and a small wasp made of coloured glass. You pocket the Gold Pieces and say to Littlebig, 'Do you think this is a magic ring?' Littlebig frowns and says, 'I'm sure it is but I have no idea what it does. Maybe if you put it on we'll be attacked by a swarm of wasps! You can't expect a nice gift from an Evil Wizard.'

If you want to try on the ring, turn to **72**.

If you want to break the glass wasp, turn to **171**.

If you would rather leave the items and continue walking up the passage, turn to **291**.

114

The bag contains: 2 Gold Pieces, a small copper bowl, a long tooth, a scroll, a wooden catapult and three lead balls. You decide to keep the gold and the catapult. If you want to look at the scroll, turn to **16**. If you would rather not look at it, you may, if you have not done so already, uncork the flask (turn to **245**) or take the sword (turn to **358**). The only other choice is to disregard the items and walk on, turn to **212**.

115

You feel groggy and extremely weak as the snake's venom spreads through your body. You lie down on the floor and start to tremble uncontrollably. Sweat pours from your brow. Standing over you, the Witch starts to laugh manically. The poison acts fast and everything goes black. Your adventure is over.

116

You walk hastily up the corridor and see an iron gate in the right-hand wall. Through the bars you can see a room which is painted entirely green. Even the tables and chairs are painted green. The room is filled with hundreds of tall plants, which give off an unpleasant smell. If you want to open the gate and enter the room, turn to **343**. If you would rather keep on walking up the corridor, turn to **142**.

117

After removing the stopper you see that the bottle contains a clear liquid. You sniff the bottle and smell something that reminds you of almonds. If you want to drink the liquid, turn to **328**. If you would rather leave it and walk on, turn to **376**.

118

The spider drops to the floor and, before it can jump up again, you stamp down on its bloated abdomen with your foot to make a green sticky mess on the floor. You are pleased to see that Littlebig has also squashed the spider that attacked him. He stands on his tiptoes, leans over the edge of the barrel and reaches down. First, he throws out a good length of rope that you decide to keep. Then he pulls himself back out again, huffing and puffing, clutching a red clay doll that has copper nails sticking out of its head like hair. 'I wonder what this is?' he asks, handing it to you. If you want to drop the doll on to the floor to break it, turn to **19**. If you would rather toss it back in the barrel and walk back down the corridor, turn to **234**.

119

The door opens and you are surprised to see what looks to be a small art gallery. The walls are almost totally covered with paintings of animals and birds. In the middle of the room an old man is busily painting a picture of a wolf on a large canvas and he is oblivious to the fact that you have come in. He just stands there humming happily to himself while he works. If you want to talk to the artist, turn to **196**. If you think he is a danger and want to attack him, turn to **348**. If you would rather leave him alone and return to the corridor, turn to **236**.

120

The cave wall is almost vertical, but there are plenty of cracks and rock outcrops to use as hand and foot holds. Nevertheless, it's going to be a difficult climb down. Roll two dice. If the number rolled is the same or less than your current SKILL score, turn to **305**. If the number rolled is greater than your SKILL score, turn to **137**.

121

The helmet does indeed have magical properties, but not the kind you were hoping for. It has been cursed by an evil sorcerer and drains the life out of anybody who wears it without them even knowing it. If you are wearing a snake's head necklace, turn to **331**. If you are not wearing this necklace, turn to **90**.

122

If you are wearing a silver armband, turn to **342**. If you are not wearing a silver armband, turn to **61**.

123

In the safety of the den, you relax and share tales of adventure with Littlebig over plates piled high with delicious food. When you can eat no more, you flop on to your bed and sink into a deep sleep, dreaming, as always, of the golden dragon. Many hours later you wake feeling strong and filled with energy. Add 4 STAMINA points. Littlebig is already sitting at the table eating another plateful of food. 'I wonder if it is breakfast or dinner time?' he asks with his cheeks bulging. 'I've completely lost track of time in this dungeon, so I'm having breakfast and dinner!' All you can manage at this point is an apple that you eat whilst having a good look around the den. A wooden box that has been tucked under one of the beds looks intriguing. You pull it out and open it to find part of an old hand-drawn map of a dungeon. It shows a section of corridor that ends at a junction where a white star is marked in chalk on the wall. An arrow pointing to the right-hand corridor has the word 'life' written underneath it and an arrow pointing to the left-hand corridor has the word 'death' written underneath it. You fold the map, place it in your pocket and tell Littlebig it's time to go. Leaving the den you turn left. Turn to 330.

124

The corridor makes a sharp turn to the right and once around the bend you are forced to stop at a deep pit. A rope hangs down from the ceiling over the centre of the pit, which you can just reach with your sword. If you want to try to swing over the pit on the rope, turn to 74. If you would rather try to jump over the pit, turn to 306.

125

Although the Hanging Snake is quick to strike, you are quicker. Your sword cuts through the air and lops off the tail end of the snake. You slide down until you reach the severed tail. It is only a two-metre jump down to the floor, and Littlebig stands beneath you to help break your fall. The wounded snake slowly rises into the ceiling to recover in its lair. You may now have a rest (turn to 314) or follow the wall around the cavern (turn to 40).

126

With your weapons at the ready, you tread carefully along the passageway. You can hardly see a metre in front of you in the thick, swirling mist, but you hear something that sounds like shuffling feet coming towards you. Littlebig raises his arm as a sign for you to stop walking. The shuffling sounds grow louder until a horrific-looking creature steps into view. It is a large, muscular humanoid that has a hunchback and an oversized head. Drool pours out of its gaping mouth that houses large broken teeth. It is its large single eye that makes it instantly recognizable. Raising its massive battleaxe above its head, the gruesome CYCLOPS strides forward to attack.

CYCLOPS   SKILL 9   STAMINA 9

If you win, turn to 200.

127

Using your sword to poke around the debris on the floor, you find 2 Gold Pieces, a silver armband and a dark blue glass bottle with a cork in it. The rotten smell in the cavern is almost unbearable and you must decide what to do. If you want to uncork the bottle, turn to **149**. If you have not done so already, you can search the bodies, turn to **299**. If you want to leave the stinking cavern immediately, turn to **76**.

128

Confident that you have made the right choice, you step forward to pull the sword from the wall. Turn to **185**.

129

You pick up the card and it springs out of your hand landing back on the floor. There is a sudden flash of blinding light. The card disappears and standing before you, from out of nowhere, is an old woman dressed as the Queen of Spades. She smiles and says, 'Thank you so much. Here are 5 Gold Pieces for your trouble.' She hands you the gold before walking slowly and elegantly out of the room. Still somewhat puzzled, you put the coins in your backpack and continue your quest. Turn to **112**.

130

The walls grind steadily on until no more than a metre separates them. You try wedging your swords between them but they snap like twigs under the pressure. There is no stopping the force that is driving the walls together. Moments later a terrible end befalls you as the walls connect. Your adventure ends here.

131

The chest lid is very heavy and you struggle to lift it. Inside you find 5 Gold Pieces, a small silver box and a strange, bronze-handled dagger with a blade made of opaque crystal. After taking what you want, you leave the chamber and continue up the corridor. Turn to **317**.

132

The fireball crashes into your chest and you are engulfed by flame. Littlebig is unable to help as the flames surround your body. As you begin to lose consciousness you see him hurled to the floor as another fireball successfully hits its target. Your adventure is over.

133

Lying still on the floor, the lifeless Gigantus once more resembles a boulder. Littlebig crouches down by its head and says, 'I'm told these spiked horns can pierce anything, even rock. They could be very useful. Maybe I should break off a few of them and put them in my backpack?' If you want to let Littlebig chop off the horns, turn to **46**. If you would rather dissuade him from doing so and continue looking for a way out of the cave, turn to **199**.

134

In the left-hand wall of the corridor you see a door which has been painted red. You hear laughter coming from the other side. It sounds like a man chuckling to himself. If you wish to open the door, turn to **374**. If you would rather walk on, turn to **65**.

135

As you step down the ladder it gets darker and darker until you can hardly see your own hands on the rungs. Looking up you can just about see Littlebig's round face beaming down at you. Down and down you go until your foot hits the floor. Suddenly you feel something crawling up your leg and then you feel lots of things crawling all over you. You feel a sting in your leg and another in your arm. You panic and try to brush the unseen attackers off your body. But there are literally hundreds of large scorpions and spiders at the bottom of the pit and they are all in a state of frenzy. There is nothing you can do but try to climb back up the ladder. Roll two dice. This is the number of STAMINA points you must lose due to poisonous stings and bites. If you are still alive, you just manage to crawl out of the pit with the help of Littlebig. If you possess Stinger Leaves, turn to **247**. If you do not have any, you may either walk on (turn to **4**) or walk back to the staircase in the cavern wall (turn to **318**).

136

You soon arrive at another alcove in the left-hand wall. Inside it you see a stone throne, carved as though it has been made out of a hundred open-mouthed skulls. If you want to sit on the throne, turn to **170**. If you would rather carry on walking up the corridor, turn to **9**.

137

You manage to climb down roughly five metres when the rock outcrop that you are standing on breaks off. You lose your footing and are left dangling helplessly by one hand. Rock fragments clatter down the side of the wall and land noisily on the floor some six metres below. Your heart starts to beat faster when you see the dragon stir. It opens one giant eye and looks around its lair, spotting you immediately. You have no choice but to jump down and face the dragon. You twist your ankle on landing and lose 1 STAMINA point.

BLACK DRAGON   SKILL 14   STAMINA 18

The dragon will concentrate its attack on you, but you will have two strikes each Attack Round, one for yourself and one for Littlebig. During the first Attack Round you must *Test your Luck* to see if you are caught within the cloud of poisonous gas that the dragon blows at you. If you are Lucky, it misses. If you are Unlucky, lose 4 STAMINA points. If somehow you manage to defeat the mighty dragon, turn to **337**.

138

Holding the lion charm in your outstretched hand, you advance towards the Wizard. When he catches sight of the charm, the Wizard begins to roar with laughter. 'Oh you pathetic weasel,' he snorts. 'What harm do you think you are going to do to me with that piece of junk?' He raises his arms and mutters a spell to release another fireball at you from point blank range. Roll two dice. If the number rolled is less than or equal to your SKILL score, turn to **267**. If the number rolled is greater than your SKILL, turn to **216**.

139

The corridor eventually comes to an end at a solid oak door. You try the handle and are surprised to find that it is unlocked. Slowly, you open the door into a dark room. The only light inside comes from a burning candle on a shelf on the far wall. Something else on the shelf also catches your eye as it sparkles in the candlelight. If you want to examine the sparkling object, turn to **381**. If you would rather close the door and walk back down the corridor, turn to **365**.

140

Inside the bag you find a small bronze statuette of a monkey with its hand covering its eyes. After deciding whether or not to keep the statuette, you set off again. If you want to go down the left-hand passage, turn to **169**. If you want to go down the right-hand passage, turn to **286**.

141

The door opens into a dark and dingy room that is covered from ceiling to floor in thick cobwebs. There doesn't appear to be anything of interest in the room. If you want to cut through the cobwebs and search the room, turn to **257**. If you want to leave the room, you may either open the door with the blue triangle (turn to **53**) or walk on up the corridor (turn to **70**).

142

Ahead in the corridor you see a stone archway, its centre stone is carved in the shape of a skull. There is a second archway another twenty metres beyond the first and there are two alcoves in between. Standing motionless in the alcoves are two tall skeletons armed with swords, helmets and shields. With your sword drawn you step slowly under the first archway. As you do so the skeletons' heads crane towards you. If you want to try to run past them, turn to **403**. If you would rather stand and fight, turn to **45**.

143

While you are cutting through the warrior's belt to take the leather bag, you feel a sharp pain in your right hand. In the gloom of the corridor you hadn't noticed that the warrior's tunic was riddled with fat, maggot-like, flesh-eating worms. Although blind, the acute sense of smell of a FLESH GRUB enables it to target its prey and sink its barbed teeth into exposed flesh. Although these vicious grubs can be pulled off and crushed easily, the number that attack can be a problem. Roll one die and add 6 to the total. This is the number of Flesh Grubs that crawl on to you. Roll two dice to decide how many you kill. If this total is less than the number of Flesh Grubs, turn to **271**. If the total is the same or greater than the number of Flesh Grubs, turn to **102**.

144

You are soon back at the sand pit and turn left to arrive at a junction in the corridor. While contemplating which way to go you notice three silver coins on the floor almost hidden in shadow. You pick them up and put them in your pocket. Having walked up the passageway to your left, you now choose to walk straight on. Turn to **304**.

145

You play your favourite tune on the tin whistle but the Ghost continues to attack Littlebig. The Ghost's sword flashes through the air and it is all Littlebig can do to defend himself. 'Stop playing that silly whistle and come and help me,' he shouts. If you have a Golden Orb and want to try that, turn to **347**. If you would rather attack the Ghost, turn to **27**.

146

A search of the room reveals nothing of interest and so you decide to search the Goblin. You landed some mighty blows on its chest during the battle, which seemed to have little effect on the Goblin. You discover that it is wearing a chain-mail coat under its clothing. It is made of a strange, blue-grey metal and you decide to put it on. Add 1 SKILL point. You leave the room and continue up the corridor. Turn to **173**.

147

You rummage through the Mercenary's pockets and find: 2 Gold Pieces, a fish hook, a small brass bell and three copper buttons. A search of the Uglukk Orc's clothing reveals nothing but maggots and lice. The unbearable smell of the cavern is beginning to make you feel sick so you decide to leave without further delay. Turn to **76**.

148

At the back of the room you find a large wooden box set against the wall that was hidden from view by the cobwebs. Littlebig looks at it closely in case it has been set as a trap. 'It doesn't look like a trap to me,' he says confidently. If you want to open the box, turn to **289**. If you would rather move the box away from the wall, turn to **326**.

149

As you uncork the bottle, wisps of shimmering white smoke escape and begin to take the shape of a man. Sitting in mid-air, on a floating silk cushion, is a short fat man with his arms folded and a turban on his head. He is semi-transparent and you can see through him. He smiles at you and says, 'Did you know that I have been stuck in that infernal bottle for over two hundred years? I cannot tell you how pleased and grateful I am to be free. I should never have trusted those tricksters. Bah! Now how can I help you, young adventurer? Would you like some gold pieces (turn to **252**) or a little magic item (turn to **67**)?'

150

The water has a metallic taste but is nevertheless quite refreshing. Add 1 STAMINA point. Strangely, your eyesight seems to have improved. Everything appears sharper and you can see further into the gloom. Littlebig also drinks the water and is overjoyed with his improved vision. 'Things are looking up,' he says setting off again. Turn to **301**.

151

Back in the corridor you arrive at another doorway in the left-hand wall. You press your ear against the wooden door and hear the sound of a woman's voice crying for help. If you want to enter the room, turn to **225**. If you want to ignore the cries and walk on, turn to **116**.

152

You are exhausted after the fight and sit down to get your breath back. Meanwhile, Littlebig starts inspecting all the swords. But as soon as he touches one of them the ghostly figure moves again and starts to attack Littlebig. You run to his aid, but at the same time wonder how you can defeat a GHOST. If only you could remember the two words that Floresto used. But you can't, so you must decide quickly what to do. If you want to try one of your items against the Ghost, turn to **187**. If you would rather attack the Ghost, turn to **27**.

153

The deep voice continues, slowly saying, 'I'm so grateful that you have decided to stay, my friend, as I am very lonely and in much need of conversation. I am a wizard trapped in another dimension. Don't ask me how I got here as it's a long story, and not a particularly nice story either. Anyway, what brings you to this evil place?' If you want to tell the wizard about your quest for the golden dragon, turn to **109**. If you would rather make a polite excuse and leave the room, turn to **264**.

154

The whispering voice continues to call to you as you reach the door and turn the handle. You enter the room cautiously and see that it is small and empty, apart from a marble plinth in the centre of a marble floor. On top of the plinth sits a highly varnished black box from which the voice appears to be coming. If you want to open the box, turn to 25. If you would rather leave the room and walk towards the opposite door, turn to 284.

155

As you walk back to the rope ladder, you stumble over something on the floor. You reach down and pick up a heavy shield. You sling it over your shoulder and climb back up the ladder on to the bridge. In the dim light of the corridor you see that the shield is etched with strange runes around its edge, and it has been polished so much that you can see your own reflection in it. You feel it was worth fighting the Ghoul after all to get such a magnificent shield and set off down the corridor. Turn to 193.

156

The corridor turns sharply right and around the corner you see an iron lever set in the left-hand wall. Littlebig looks at it carefully but does not touch it. 'Could be a trap,' he says, again stating the obvious in his now familiar way. If you want to pull down on the handle, turn to 366. If you would rather just keep walking, turn to 44.

157

You close both hands around the shaft of the arrow and pull on it as hard as you can. The arrowhead remains firmly embedded in the rock wall. You try again but you are unable to move it. Turn to **38**.

158

You say hello to the old woman and yet she still does not turn around to look at you. You decide to walk up to her and tap her on the shoulder. Suddenly she spins around. Her eyes are wide open with glee and an evil, hysterical laugh erupts from her mouth. Close up you notice that she has tiny snakes in her hair and realize in horror that she must be a MEDUSA. You try to avoid her staring eyes by looking away as you know her gaze is deadly. Roll two dice. If the total is the same or less than your SKILL, you avoid her stare. If you are carrying a piece of broken mirror you may be able to reflect her stare back at her, turn to **210**. If you do not have this item, you can run out of the room, turn to **281**. If the total is greater than your SKILL you catch sight of her deadly gaze, turn to **377**.

159

If you have any keys, turn to **276**. If you do not have any keys, turn to **259**.

160

Littlebig frowns and says, 'I've got a feeling that this is not such a good idea.' But you ignore his words and run at the old man with your sword raised. You are almost within striking distance when the old man leaps up and instantly metamorphoses into a horrific beast almost three metres high and covered in scaly black skin. Steam hisses from its nostrils and a terrible stench of foul breath blows out of its fanged mouth. It has a large head with long horns curving out of the top. Its hands end in hooked claws. It has cloven hooves and a long, lashing tail. You are face to face with a raging HELL DEMON and you realize that your sword will cause it no harm. It fends off your blow with ease and strikes back with its iron-like claws. Lose 2 STAMINA points. You reel back from the blow and hear Littlebig shouting something from behind you. You just catch the words 'wavy blade' and they puzzle you. Suddenly the words make sense. If you have a kris knife, turn to **195**. If you do not have this knife, turn to **371**.

161

In the heat of battle you suddenly notice that somebody else has entered the room. It is a huge bearded man, wearing thick leather armour reinforced with steel shoulder pads. 'Pay me 10 Gold Pieces and I will help you,' he growls in a deep voice. If you want to agree to the Mercenary's demands, turn to **334**. If you would rather tell him that you do not need his help, turn to **213**.

162

Lo Lo Mai's pleasant smile disappears from her face and in a stern voice she says,

'Your words are false, that I know,
It's your mistake, now you must go.'

She walks quickly over to the door opposite and opens it, gesturing for you to walk through. Something tells you that it would be foolish to disobey her, so you do as she says. Turn to **396**.

163

While their evil power and near-immortality make Vampires very difficult to kill, silver weapons can harm them. You plunge the dagger into her chest and watch on in amazement as her body crumbles into dust. A bat emerges from the dust and flies away, carrying with it the Vampire's spirit. In two days time the Vampire will return in human form and will come looking for you to exact her revenge. Suddenly you notice something else lying in the pile of dust – a jewel on a gold chain. The jewel is an emerald, but, much to your disappointment, it is square and not shaped like a dragon's eye at all. You place it quickly in the black pouch in your pocket and leave the room in a great deal of excitement. Turn to **116**.

164

You swerve around the clawed hand of the Zombie and run off into the gloom of the cavern. The lumbering Zombies are soon left far behind. Turn to **376**.

165

The few pages remaining in the old book are yellow and brittle. The ink writing on them is very faded and almost illegible, but on the last page there is a rhyme which looks to have been written in blood. If you want to read the rhyme, turn to **260**. Alternatively, if you have not done so already, you may either open the wooden chest (turn to **327**) or strike the staff on the floor (turn to **198**). You may also walk on and follow the arrows along the corridor, turn to **248**.

166

The corridor is long and narrow with just the occasional burning torch on the wall to light the way. You walk along slowly, ever alert to potential danger. A rat suddenly scurries across the damp floor before disappearing into a hole in the wall. On and on you walk, until you hear the sound of flowing water in the distance. The corridor eventually ends at the bank of a fast-flowing underground river. A crudely made raft is tied to a stake in the bank. If you want to climb on to the raft and float downstream, turn to **188**. If you would rather retrace your steps and walk back to the last junction, turn to **398**.

167

The door opens into a marble-floored room in the middle of which stands an ornate stone table. Two shining breastplates lie on top of the table, one is made of bronze and the other is made of iron. If you want to try on the bronze breastplate, turn to **3**. If want to try on the iron breastplate, turn to **37**. If you do not wish to try on either, you leave the room and continue up the corridor. Turn to **151**.

168

You rummage frantically through your backpack in a desperate search for the healing potion. Finally you find it just in time as you begin to feel weak. You gulp down all of the potion and sit down on the floor to rest for a while. You soon feel better and well enough to continue. Turn to **148**.

169

Littlebig notices something on the floor and runs ahead to investigate. It's a large stone chest some two metres long with a very heavy-looking lid. 'Funny place to leave this,' Littlebig says, stating the blindingly obvious. 'I wonder what's inside?' If you want to try to lift the lid off the chest, turn to **35**. If you would rather walk on, turn to **156**.

170

Sensing a trap, you sit down very slowly on the chair. You think you hear the sound of wailing voices but realize it's just your imagination. Suddenly, a feeling of incredible power surges through your body. You are sitting on a chair of life. Add 1 SKILL point and 1 STAMINA point. Feeling strong, you leap out of the chair and stride up the corridor, turn to **9**.

171

You drop the glass wasp on the stone floor but it doesn't break. You stamp on it with your foot but still it doesn't break. You even try smashing it with the hilt of your sword but that does not work. 'Give it to me,' says Littlebig. 'I'm going to keep it. It might be a lucky charm after all.' You toss it over to him and decide what to do. If you have not done so already, you may try on the ring (turn to **72**) or continue walking up the passage (turn to **291**).

172

As the Verminspawn gets closer, you feel almost paralysed by fear, and looking at the insects and grubs crawling over its loathsome torso makes you feel sick. It is all you can do to raise your sword to fight. But fight you must.

VERMINSPAWN   SKILL 10   STAMINA 10

During this combat, you must reduce your SKILL by 3 because of your fear. Littlebig is unable to move at all and stands motionless with his mouth wide open. If somehow you manage to win, turn to **380**.

173

The dank and gloomy corridor finally ends at a doorway. As you are deciding whether or not to open it, you hear a noise like that of grating metal followed by the loud clang of metal hitting stone. You look around to see that your way back is barred by an iron bar gate that has dropped down from the ceiling. You have no choice but to turn the door handle. You find yourself in a marble-floored room. The room is empty but there are a pair of golden footprints in a silver circle on the floor. A sign on the wall says 'Please stand on the footprints'. From out of nowhere you hear the sound of thunder followed by a loud evil laugh. If you want to stand on the footprints, turn to **302**. If you want to wait and see if the owner of the evil laugh will appear, turn to **103**.

174

One of the pointed darts sinks into your thigh. As you reach down to pull it out you begin to feel very dizzy. The tips of the darts have been coated with deadly poison by a gang of dungeon looters. It will not be long before they return to rob your lifeless body of all your treasure. Your adventure ends here.

175

All of the magic keys have a number stamped on them. To open a box, turn to the paragraph number that is stamped on the key you wish to try first. If you are unable to do this, you will just have to guess which weapon to choose. Turn to **390**.

176

You enter a room that is painted white which contains white furniture and objects. In a corner of the room, standing on a white marble column, you see a cat made of white porcelain that has jewelled eyes. If you want to take a closer look at the cat, turn to **383**. If you would rather leave the room straight away, turn to **204**.

177

If you have any of the following magic items, you may choose to use one now.

Lion Charm.	Turn to **138**
Moonstone Brooch.	Turn to **52**
Staff of Thunder.	Turn to **333**

If you do not have any of these items you can either attack the Evil Wizard with your sword (turn to **320**) or offer him some Gold Pieces (turn to **96**).

178

As you draw your sword from the body of the last Zombie, you look around to see that Littlebig has already despatched his two Zombies and is rummaging through their pockets. He finds a leather pouch, which he hands to you. If you want to open the pouch, turn to **287**. If you would rather walk on, turn to **376**.

179

As you plummet down the chute, your head bangs against a stone outcrop. Lose 3 STAMINA points. If you are still alive, turn to **105**.

180

The Hell Demon swipes at you with its razor-sharp claws and catches you on the head as you run past. If you are wearing a helmet, lose 1 STAMINA point only. If you are not wearing a helmet, lose 4 STAMINA points from the deep head wound caused. If you are still alive, you summon all your remaining energy and run for your life. Turn to **286**.

181

You feel a tingling sensation as the liquid runs down your throat. A dull pain that starts in your stomach quickly spreads through your body. If you are wearing a turquoise ring, turn to **82**. If you are not wearing this ring, turn to **332**.

182

Furiously hacking, stamping, crushing and stabbing, you attack the swarm of Plague Rats. Inevitably some of them will bite you, as there are 37 of them! Each Attack Round roll one die and add your current SKILL score to it. This is the number of rats you kill each round. Each round that any are left alive, you will lose 1 STAMINA point. If you win, turn to **57**.

183

As the walls close in, you just have time to jump through the hole in the wall to avoid being crushed. You land heavily on the floor of an enormous cave. Water drops noisily on to the floor from the tips of stalactites hanging down from the high rock ceiling above. The cave is lit by a strange fluorescent fungus, which grows in patches all over the walls and gives off an eerie amber light. 'I wonder if that was the emerald we were looking for?' Littlebig asks a little gloomily. 'I hope not.' You tell Littlebig not to worry and suggest he starts looking for a way out of the cave. Turn to **266**.

184

The painting is of a red dragon asleep in its cavern lair surrounded by thousands of gold pieces and items of treasure. You can hardly believe your eyes when one of the dragon's eyes flicks open and its tail swishes from side to side. Instinctively you drop the painting on the floor and draw your sword as the dragon takes on a three-dimensional shape and expands out of the painting. Smoke shoots out of its nostrils as it flaps its wings to prepare for flight. Even though it is only a metre in length, the dragon's fiery breath and sharp talons can cause a lot of damage.

RED DRAGON   SKILL 6   STAMINA 6

If you win, turn to **391**.

185

You wrap your fingers around the handle of the sword and pull it gently. You smile as the sword slides out easily from the rock as though from its scabbard. Littlebig screams with delight and grabs hold of the dagger, the last remaining weapon. It, too, comes free and both of you start to chuckle with nervous laughter as a section of the wall starts to rise into the ceiling to reveal another room. Standing on a wooden plinth, in the middle of an otherwise empty room, is a magnificent treasure made of gold. 'Look!' shouts Littlebig, almost beside himself with excitement. 'A dragon! It's the golden dragon!' With your heart pounding, you walk into the treasure chamber and stare almost in disbelief at the golden dragon that you have been seeking. Now here it is within touching distance. Your mind suddenly goes back to when you were in the Blue Pig Tavern and you recall the words of warning given to you by Henry Delacor. 'Before touching the golden dragon, place both the emerald eyes in their sockets.' If you have two emerald eyes, turn to **49**. If you only have one emerald, turn to **84**.

186

After turning sharply right, the corridor soon ends at a large oak door with ornate iron hinges The door is firmly shut. If you wish to try to force the door open, turn to **389**. If you would rather save your energy and return to the last junction to continue on, turn to **288**.

187

The Ghost has been under the spell of Floresto for over five years, acting as both a guardian for his collection of swords and also as a combat training partner. However, magical music can release this trapped soul back to its own world. If you have something musical you should use it now. Will you:

Try a Golden Orb?	Turn to **347**
Try a Tin Whistle?	Turn to **145**
Use neither of these and attack with your sword?	Turn to **27**

188

The channel narrows and the flow of the river increases. You are soon in a tunnel with a very low ceiling and are forced to lie flat on the raft. Ahead, you hear the roar of water crashing into unseen depths and you realize to your horror that you are heading for a waterfall. Suddenly the raft hits a rock and breaks apart before plunging over the edge of the waterfall. You are bowled over and over and crash into a dark, watery grave. Your adventure is over.

189

Having nothing in your possession with which to open the door, you decide to climb back down the staircase to find another way out. You spend the next few hours walking around the cavern. Littlebig starts to complain that he is tired and fed up but you keep on searching for a way out until you are quite exhausted. Finally you call it a day and lie down to sleep between two boulders. You fall into such a deep sleep that you do not hear the almost silent flutter of the wings of a Vampire Bat circling overhead. Finally it lands nearby and transforms into a female Vampire who is seeking revenge. She walks silently over to you and sinks her two fangs into your neck while you sleep. Then she does the same to Littlebig. When you wake, both of you will have become Vampires, condemned to a shadow life. Your adventure is over.

190

You just manage to scramble to the other side of the pit. As you land, some small stones are dislodged and fall back into the dark pit. You hear some shuffling sounds below and wonder what creature lurks in the shadows. Not staying to find out, you hurry on up the corridor. Turn to **98**.

191

A black rat suddenly appears out of a hole in the wall. It looks crazed, with mad red eyes and a slavering jaw from which two long fangs protrude. It runs straight at you without fear and jumps on to your leg. Roll two dice. If the total is the same or less than your SKILL, turn to 370. If the total is higher than your SKILL, turn to 66.

192

The copper key turns the lock of the copper box. It clicks open and inside you find a polished stone etched with the words 'four sword'. Turn to 227.

193

The corridor comes to an end at a junction with turnings to left and right. If you want to walk down the left-hand corridor, turn to 54. If you would rather go down the right-hand corridor, turn to 20.

194

You tread warily around the slumbering beast. Having successfully avoided waking it you enter a new tunnel. Turn to 378.

195

As the raging Hell Demon closes in for the kill, you frantically grab the fabled knife from your belt and strike out and up at the demon's throat. It tries to block the knife with its muscular arm but howls in pain as the tempered blade severs it completely, like a knife cutting through butter. Amazed and excited, you lunge at the demon again, spurred on by Littlebig's shouts of encouragement.

HELL DEMON   SKILL 10   STAMINA 10

Each time you win an Attack Round, the kris knife will cause 2 SKILL points and 4 STAMINA points of damage. If you win, turn to **232**.

196

You cough to get the attention of the old man who then puts down his brush to look at you. He enquires if he can be of assistance and you ask him if he knows the whereabouts of the emerald you are seeking. He tugs on his beard and shakes his head. 'We don't speak about the Eye of the Dragon here,' he says nervously. 'Most of those who've come treasure hunting down in the dungeons have never been seen again. Can't help you I'm afraid. But would you like to buy my new painting of a lovely owl?' he asks enthusiastically. 'I only want 5 Gold Pieces for it.' If you wish to buy the small painting you must pay his asking price before leaving the room. Or you can leave without buying the painting. Turn to **236**.

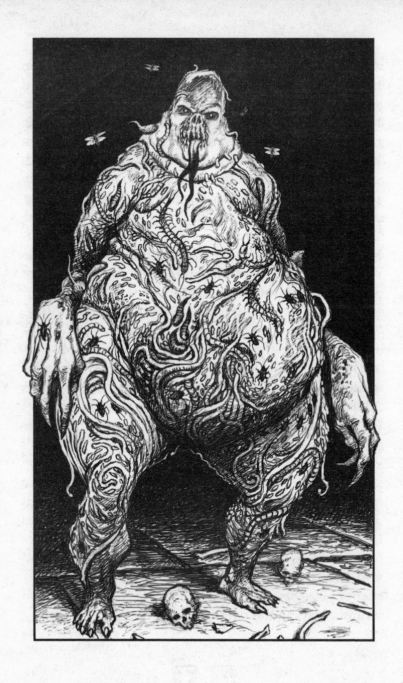

Holding a burning torch in front of him, Littlebig leads the way down the steps. You descend into a large cellar with bare stone walls that are damp and covered with brown fungus. The floor has large patches of sticky green slime covering it and old bones and skulls are everywhere. The hissing sound grows louder and suddenly the most hideous creature you have ever seen steps slowly into view from out of the shadows. Its shape is humanoid but large and blubbery. Foul green slime drips from sores on its repulsive body. But the most revolting thing about the VERMINSPAWN is that its body is completely covered by worms, lice, cockroaches, maggots, rats and leeches that crawl in and out of every orifice, crease and fold on its bloated body. A forked tongue flicks out of its gaping mouth, which houses rows of blackened teeth. The Verminspawn is a fearsome fighter and it possesses mental powers that paralyse its opponents with fear. If you have the 'Skullsplitter' sword, turn to **87**. If you do not have this sword, turn to **172**.

198

When the staff hits the stone there is a deafening boom that is louder than the loudest thunder you have ever heard. It causes a sonic wave, which knocks you off your feet when you let go of the staff. Lose 1 STAMINA point. When you pick it up to give it a closer inspection you see an inscription on it in tiny writing. It says 'Staff of Thunder – hold on tight.' You remember these words and decide to keep the staff. If you have not done so already, you may either open the wooden chest (turn to 327) or open the book (turn to 165). Alternatively you may follow the arrows down the corridor (turn to 248).

199

The noise of water dripping from the stalactites into the pool on the floor echoes eerily through the cavern. You notice that one pool has a wooden ladle lying next to it. The water in the pool seems to sparkle in the light. If you would like to drink the water, turn to 150. If you would rather keep walking, turn to 301.

200

No sooner does the lifeless body of the Cyclops hit the floor than Littlebig starts searching through its pockets. When he's finished he shakes his head and says, 'I can't believe the only things of any value this brute had were 3 Gold Pieces. But I'll take his battle-axe, thank you very much. Very nice craftsmanship, I must say.' You pocket the Gold Pieces and set off again down the misty corridor. Eventually the mist clears and you arrive at a metal door in the right-hand wall that has a sign attached to it with the words 'Pia's Potions'. If you want to open the door, turn to **393**. If you would rather walk on, turn to **265**.

201

As you plunge your sword into the Snake Witch, she disappears in a puff of smoke. You hear her sickly voice shout 'You missed!' When the smoke clears she is nowhere to be seen. A mouse runs between your feet and through a tiny hole in the far wall. Meanwhile, the cauldron starts to boil over on the fire and you see the image of the Snake Witch in the steam. Her eyes stare at you and her mouth is wide open with laughter, although you cannot hear her laugh. She extends an arm towards you, gesturing with one long crooked finger for you to come closer. In the palm of her hand you see a small emerald in the shape of an eye! Your heart skips a beat with excitement. If you want to grab the emerald from her outstretched hand, turn to **357**. If you would rather leave the room immediately, turn to **323**.

202

The dimly lit corridor comes to a dead end where there is a large wooden barrel standing against the wall. 'That's a bit of a strange place to leave a barrel,' Littlebig remarks. 'I wonder what's inside it?' If you want to prise the lid off the barrel with your sword, turn to **50**. If you would rather go back down the corridor, turn to **234**.

203

The noise of the stone is not loud enough to wake the sleeping dragon. But the look of fear on Littlebig's face is so intense you almost burst out laughing. You carry on walking on tip-toes and enter the new tunnel. Turn to **378**.

204

Striding up the corridor you see a dilapidated wooden doorway in the left-hand wall. If you want to step through the doorway, turn to **64**. If you want to keep on walking, turn to **317**.

205

You lift it carefully out of the coffin and are surprised to hear soft music coming from it. You put the orb down on the floor and the music stops. It starts again when you lift it up. You hand it to Littlebig who places it in your backpack and once again it falls silent. 'How strange,' says Littlebig. 'But I'm sure it will come in useful sometime or other. Let's go.' Littlebig strides off and you walk on after him. Turn to **156**.

206

With your sword ready for action you cautiously peer around the corner, but there is nobody to be seen. The corridor ahead ends in a T-junction where there is a white symbol on the wall. You decide to take a closer look. Turn to **308**.

207

As you run past the Skeletons you feel a sharp pain in your back. The sword of one of the Skeletons has sliced through your clothing and made a deep wound in your back. Lose 3 STAMINA points. Not stopping to look behind, you run on down the corridor. Turn to **134**.

208

As you run past the Hell Demon it lashes out at you with its claws and catches your midriff. If you are wearing chain-mail, lose 1 STAMINA point only. If you are not wearing chain-mail, lose 4 STAMINA points from the deep gash in your stomach. If you are still alive, you summon all your remaining energy and run for your life. Turn to **169**.

209

Littlebig strides on confidently and says, 'I bet that message is rubbish and the golden dragon is down here somewhere. Somebody didn't want us to follow them.' He has hardly finished speaking when suddenly the corridor floor gives way beneath your feet. You fall ten metres down a pit and land on iron spikes that are tipped with deadly poison. Your adventure is over.

210

You take the piece of mirror out of your backpack and hold it up to the Medusa. You hear an anguished scream, which quickly fades to silence. Slowly, you open one eye and then the other to see the rigid torso of the Medusa who has been turned to stone by the reflection of her own stare. You put the mirror in your backpack and search the room. In a corner cupboard you find an ornate wooden box which opens to reveal a strange necklace. A small snake's skull hangs on a silver chain. If you want to put the necklace around your neck, turn to **297**. If you would rather leave the room without it, turn to **281**.

211

The door opens into a cavernous room in which the floor is littered with small bones and debris. Standing in the middle of the debris you see an ugly two-headed TROLL. It is busy sharpening its large axe on a spinning stone wheel that is powered by a treadle. One of its head's turns to stare at you. Its face is covered with warts and its large teeth stick out of its drooling mouth like tusks. It is violent, stupid and very dangerous. If you want to fight the Troll, turn to **359**. If you would rather slam the door shut and hurry on up the corridor, turn to **166**.

212

You soon arrive at a wooden trapdoor in the floor. While you stand guard, Littlebig lifts the trapdoor by its iron ring. A horrible stench wafts up into your nostrils making you feel quite ill. Stone steps lead down into the gloom below, from where you can hear a faint hissing sound. If you want to go down the steps, turn to **197**. If you would rather close the trapdoor and walk on, turn to **355**.

213

The Mercenary grunts and turns around to walk out of the cavern. The Uglukk Orc cannot resist a chance to land a cowardly blow. Turning away from you, it strides towards the Mercenary and lands a mighty blow on his head with its heavy club. The Mercenary crumples to the floor with blood pouring from his cracked skull. Thinking this tactic is a good one to use yourself in these circumstances, you rush at the Orc from behind and strike a heavy blow with your sword. The Orc, too, slumps to the floor, its dying breath gurgling in its throat. If you want to search the bodies, turn to **299**. If you would rather search the cavern first, turn to **127**.

214

You stare at the axe for a few seconds as you convince yourself that you are making the right choice. You take hold of the axe handle in both hands and lean back to pull on it. You breathe a huge sigh of relief as the axe comes away from the wall with ease. Now there are only two weapons left in the wall. If you want to choose the sword to pull first, turn to **128**. If you want to pull the dagger first, turn to **2**.

215

Hardly able to see, and feeling sick and disorientated, you wake up in a tiny room measuring some two metres by two metres. There are no doors in the walls. On the low ceiling there is a luminous crystal, which gives off an eerie green glow. You have been teleported to an old prison cell in another part of the labyrinth. Lose 2 SKILL points and 2 STAMINA points. You scratch around in the thick dirt on the floor and find an iron bolt which is attached to what feels like it could be a trapdoor. You pull on the bolt and suddenly the iron door falls open into a room below. If you want to search further in the dirt of the prison cell, turn to **29**. If you would rather jump down into the room below, turn to **64**.

216

If you are carrying a shield, turn to **397**. If you do not have a shield, turn to **132**.

217

You utter the magical words at the top of your voice but, to your absolute horror, they fail to work. Turn to 130.

218

You stand back from the lifeless Wolf and look around. The old man has gone. A search of the room reveals a highly polished steel wristband that the old man was using as a brush holder. After placing it on your wrist you feel a sudden surge of power run through your body. Add 1 SKILL point and leave the room. Turn to 236.

219

You soon arrive at the edge of a pit that is roughly three metres square. A bamboo ladder runs down one side into total darkness. 'You won't catch me climbing down that ladder,' Littlebig says quite firmly. 'If you want to, however, be my guest!' If you want to climb down the ladder, turn to 394. If you would rather walk on, turn to 4.

220

As you walk along you notice a trail of dried blood on the floor, as though a wounded creature has been dragged along the floor. You follow the trail of blood to a door in the left-hand wall which has strange symbols crudely etched into it. Whoever was wounded must have been dragged into the room or corridor on the other side of the door. You press your ear to the door and hear the sound of somebody moaning in pain. If you want to open the door, turn to **277**. If you would rather walk on up the corridor, turn to **307**.

221

You drop to your knees as the poison takes its toll. You begin to lose consciousness and your body feels like it is on fire with fever. You can't quite believe that after all you have been through, and the creatures you have fought, a tiny spider could defeat you. Lose 7 STAMINA points. If you are still alive, turn to **349**.

222

As you start to walk, you trip over one of the Skeletons and fall to the ground. Your helmet falls off your head as you land. You immediately feel stronger, as if a bolt of energy has surged through you. You kick the helmet against the wall and you hear a sound like a cry of pain. Taking no chances, you swing a mighty blow with your sword on to the helmet, cleaving it in two. You grunt in satisfaction and walk on down the corridor. Turn to **134**.

223

The Mercenary's ugly face erupts with rage as he raises his sword with both hands high above his head, ready to strike a heavy blow. 'Nobody goes back on a deal with me and lives to see the light of day,' he screams at the top of his gruff voice. You have no choice but to fight the giant man.

MERCENARY   SKILL 8   STAMINA 10

If you win, turn to **147**.

224

You turn the corner and see the figure running away as fast as he can. 'Let him go,' Littlebig shouts, 'I'll never catch him. You can chase him on your own but don't forget to come back for me.' If you want to let the person escape, turn to 368. If you want to run after him on your own, turn to 99.

225

You walk into a large room that, much to your surprise, is crammed full of lavish furniture and furnishings. There are ornately carved tables and chairs, beautiful paintings and vases, and embroidered drapes and curtains. At the back of the room, you are shocked to see a beautiful young woman is locked inside an iron cage. She seems unafraid of you and smiles coyly. If you want to try to rescue her, turn to 10. If you wish to leave the room immediately, turn to 116.

226

Hovering above the steaming embers of the fire, the illusion of the Snake Witch reappears. She smiles and says, 'Only a fool such as you would expect to barge into my chamber and steal an emerald of such beauty. My name is Vigdis and I am the most beautiful woman in the world. Do you agree?' You look at her and are repulsed by her hideous face, which is covered with scabs and warts. Her nose is long and hairy, and her mouth houses two rows of broken black teeth. If you wish to agree with her, turn to 71. If you want to tell her she is ugly, turn to 100.

227

If you have another key and you wish to open another box, turn to the number that is stamped on the key. If you have finished opening the boxes or do not have any more keys, turn to 390.

228

You are consumed by a raging temperature and your vision is badly blurred. You sink to your knees feeling as though you cannot move a muscle. You expect to feel the sharp pain of the spider's bite again but instead you feel cold liquid hit your face and then somebody pushing some foul-tasting leaves into your mouth. 'Come on young adventurer,' shouts Littlebig. 'It's no time to go to sleep now. Chewing these lumbugg leaves will soon have you feeling as fit as a flea,' he laughs, quite unconcerned that you feel as though you are about to die. It only takes a few minutes for the leaves to counteract the poison. The fever is gone and you feel fine again. Add 2 STAMINA points. You stand up and see two squashed spiders on the floor that must have been stamped on by Littlebig, who is now standing on his tiptoes trying to reach down into the barrel. First, he throws out a good length of rope that you decide to keep. Then he pulls himself back out again huffing and puffing, clutching a red clay doll that has copper nails sticking out of its head like hair. 'I wonder what this is?' asks Littlebig, handing it to you. If you want to drop the doll on to the floor to break it, turn to 19. If you would rather throw it back in the barrel and walk back down the corridor, turn to 234.

229

After wiping the blood from your sword you begin a search of the kitchen. There are lots of utensils, pots and pans but nothing of use to you. You are about to leave when you notice a corked green bottle on top of a cupboard. You pick it up and uncork it to find that it contains a clear, odourless liquid. If you want to drink some of the liquid, turn to **32**. If you would rather pour it away, leave the kitchen and continue up the corridor, turn to **336**.

230

There is nothing of interest in the cellar but you find an iron door in the far corner. It is not locked but it is very heavy and difficult to open due to its rusted hinges. If you want to open it fully, turn to **104**. If you would rather leave the cellar and continue along the corridor above, turn to **355**.

231

As you climb up into their lair, another of the Niblicks lands its club on the back of your head. If you are wearing a helmet, lose 1 STAMINA point. If you are not wearing a helmet, lose 3 STAMINA points. Bruised and battered you draw your sword to fight the Niblicks one at a time.

	SKILL	STAMINA
First NIBLICK	4	3
Second NIBLICK	5	2
Third NIBLICK	3	4

If you win, turn to **295**.

232

Littlebig looks down at the bloody corpse and says, 'How did that thing find a way to our world? It must have killed and eaten the poor old man and taken his image to roam through the dungeon looking harmless. It's a good thing that you had the kris knife or we would have been eaten too.' Littlebig points to the floor and says, 'Hey, what's that on the floor under the chair?' You look to where he is pointing and see a leather bag. Will you:

Open the leather bag?	Turn to **140**
Leave it and go down the left-hand passage?	Turn to **169**
Leave it and go down the right-hand passage?	Turn to **286**

233

You tell Littlebig that you will enter first and bend down to crawl along the dark tunnel. In the far distance you can see a faint glow of light and, as you approach the end of the tunnel, you try to be as quiet as possible. You see that it opens out into a huge cave and that you are halfway up the side of the wall. Looking down, you see a giant, black-scaled reptile asleep in the middle of the floor. It has a long neck and tail and huge wings that are folded across its ridged back. Smoke rises from its large, gaping nostrils. There is no mistaking it: the terrifying beast that is slumbering below is a BLACK DRAGON. 'Maybe we can creep past it while it's asleep,' whispers Littlebig. 'But how are we going to get down on to the floor of the dragon's lair?' If you are carrying a coil of rope, turn to **242**. If you do not have any rope, you will have to climb down the wall. Turn to **120**.

234

As you walk back along the corridor you suddenly see something in the wall that you hadn't noticed earlier. It's a small hole, just big enough to put your hand into. If you want to reach into the hole, turn to **101**. If you would rather keep walking back to the junction and head straight on, turn to **354**.

235

Lo Lo Mai looks suddenly excited and says,

> *'The room of webs might seem bare*
> *But you'll find a secret tunnel there*
> *Beyond the weapons fixed in stone*
> *The golden dragon stands alone.'*

Without further ado, she walks over to the door opposite and opens it, gesturing for you to walk through it. Trusting her, you do as she bids. Turn to **396**.

236

You soon arrive at another doorway in the right-hand wall and above it there is a sign which reads 'Thomas Cornpepper, Merchant'. If you wish to open the door, turn to **329**. If you want to continue walking up the corridor, turn to **262**.

237

You see that there is now thick slimy jelly running down the walls, large globules of the stuff are falling off the ceiling and landing on the floor with a dull splat sound. The jelly is green and vapour rises from it. The acid smell is quite intense and unpleasant to breathe. Littlebig pokes his dagger into the jelly and there is a loud hissing sound as it dissolves the tip of the blade. 'Death Slime,' Littlebig mumbles to himself, 'I've heard about it but I've never seen it before. Believe it or not, this stuff is alive. It can reform into one ball of slime and even take a humanoid shape to attack and consume you. We have got to go quickly before it does. If you get a drop of this stuff on you it will burn a hole right through you!' If you want to make a run for it past the Death Slime, turn to **356**. If you want to turn around again and walk through the mist, turn to **126**.

238

As you walk along the corridor, two rats run past you and disappear into a small hole in the left-hand wall. Another rat appears in front of you, it stops when it sees you and scurries into the hole in the wall. In the distance you can see that the floor is littered with broken bones that are being gnawed on by ten or eleven rats. As you get closer, you can see that the bones are definitely humanoid. 'Somebody met an untimely end here,' says Littlebig rather sombrely. Suddenly he runs towards the rats, screaming at the top of his voice. The rats scatter and run off in all directions, leaving Littlebig standing among the bones looking rather solemn. You ask him why he is looking so glum. He points at a brass button on the floor and says, 'This button has a special symbol of a letter S with a crown above it. That means it comes from Stonebridge, my village. But I wonder who it belonged to? I'm going to take it with me in case somebody back home recognizes it.' You pat Littlebig reassuringly on the back and suggest you move on.

You soon come to an old iron door in the left-hand wall that is firmly locked from the inside. There is no keyhole. Littlebig gives it a couple of kicks with his large boots just for good measure, but it doesn't budge. Suddenly, a figure appears from around the corner in the distance, sees you, and disappears back around the corner. If you want to chase after the figure, turn to **92**. If you want to continue trying to open the door, turn to **404**.

239

The pendant feels warm against your skin and it also gives off a faint green glow. If you want to take off the pendant, leave the room and walk back down the corridor, turn to **365**. If you would rather leave the pendant on, turn to **62**.

240

All of the sheets of paper have a two-line rhyme written on them in red ink. Some of the rhymes have lines drawn through them as if they have been discarded. None of them make sense to you or Littlebig, apart from one which reads:

> *'If you see a monster double,*
> *The left one is the cause of trouble.'*

Littlebig frowns and says, 'That must mean there is a deadly Doppelgänger somewhere in this dungeon. They are able to transform themselves into a duplicate image of any humanoid near them, and if you attack the person being copied instead of the Doppelgänger itself, well, you could lose friends that way! But now we know, don't we!' Thinking about the Doppelgänger, you decide what to do. If you have not done so already, you may drink the soup (turn to **89**). Otherwise you can open the door opposite (turn to **312**).

241

The Witch starts shrieking at the top of her voice, 'Dim and Dumb, my little boys! You've killed Dim and Dumb. Now you are going to pay for this with your own life!' She suddenly reaches down to open a trapdoor and cackles with glee as a swarm of black rats jump out of the hole to attack you. If you are wearing a gold bracelet, turn to **12**. If you are not wearing a gold bracelet, turn to **182**.

242

After fixing the rope to a rock overhang, you lower yourself over the edge with Littlebig following right behind. Turn to **305**.

243

The door opens into another dimly lit, stone-walled passageway which ends at a doorway. The door is not locked and you enter a small, circular room with a shallow pool at its centre. A ledge around the pool allows you to walk to the closed door opposite you. At the bottom of the pool lie several gold coins. If you want to throw one of your Gold Pieces into the pool and make a wish, turn to **15**. If you would rather walk around to the far door, turn to **322**.

244

As soon as you touch your sword there is a blinding flash and, momentarily, you are unable to see anything. When your sight returns it is blurred, and everything looks slightly out of focus. Lose 1 SKILL point. Pia and her potions are nowhere to be seen. 'I think she disappeared through a secret door at the back of the room,' Littlebig says, rubbing his eyes. You try to find a way to open the secret door but eventually give up. There is nothing you can do but leave the room. Turn to **265**.

245

There is a clear liquid inside the silver flask that has a faint odour of herbs. If you want to drink the liquid, turn to **181**. If you would rather not chance it, you may, if you have not done so already, either open the leather bag (turn to **114**) or take the sword (turn to **358**). Your only other option is to walk on (turn to **212**).

246

You are too quick for the Skeletons. Their swords slice through the air but fail to hit you. Without looking behind, you run through the second alcove and on down the corridor. Turn to **134**.

247

Littlebig helps you rub the healing Stinger Leaves on to your bites and stings. You use them all up, but they do help to counteract the insects' poison. Add 4 STAMINA points. 'So what are we going to do now?' asks Littlebig. If you want to walk on, turn to **4**. If you would rather walk back to the staircase in the cavern wall, turn to **318**.

248

You follow the chalk arrows until the corridor comes to a dead end where you see a chalk circle on the floor. Hanging through a hole in the ceiling above the circle is a thick rope. If you want to pull on the rope, turn to **350**. If you would rather walk back down the corridor, turn to **144**.

249

You smile and introduce yourself and Littlebig to Lo Lo Mai. She smiles back at you and says,

> *'Welcome warriors brave and bold*
> *Do you seek the dragon made of gold?'*

If you want to reply 'yes', turn to **235**. If you want to reply 'no', turn to **162**.

250

The corridor turns sharply to the left and continues straight on. Further on you come to a wooden door in the right-hand wall that has a bright yellow painting of a sun in the middle of it. You listen at the door but hear nothing. If you want to open the door, turn to **176**. If you wish to continue walking up the corridor, turn to **204**.

251

You convince yourself that the dagger is the correct choice and step forward to pull it from the wall. You feel your heart beating faster as you reach out to take the dagger. Turn to **280**.

252

The fat man suddenly disappears in a puff of smoke and is replaced on the cushion by a knotted leather purse. You take the purse, untie the knot and count 15 Gold Pieces into your hand. Add 1 LUCK point. If you have not done so already you may search the bodies (turn to **299**) or leave the cavern (turn to **76**).

253

There is a pack of rats gnawing on the bones that you see, as you approach, are definitely humanoid. 'Somebody met an untimely end here,' says Littlebig, rather sombrely. Suddenly he runs towards the rats, screaming at the top of his voice. The rats scatter and run off in all directions, leaving Littlebig standing amid the bones looking rather solemn. You ask him why he is looking so glum. He points at a brass button on the floor and says, 'This button has a special symbol of a letter S with a crown above it. That means it comes from Stonebridge, my village. But I wonder who it belonged to? I'm going to take it with me in case somebody back home recognizes it. Maybe that person we saw just now knows something about it. I suggest we go and find out.' If you want to turn around and chase after the figure, turn to **92**. If you would rather keep on walking, turn to **191**.

254

You enter a dingy, cramped room. The walls are lined with shelves that are stacked with all sorts of bottles and jars containing herbs, potions, insects, dead rats and disgusting-looking things like pickled ears and animal droppings. A huge fire is burning in the centre of the room, over which an ugly old woman with long black fingernails is stirring foul-smelling sludge in a cauldron. She turns to face you and smiles to reveal two rows of broken black teeth. If you want to talk to her, turn to **95**. If you would rather leave the room without talking to the woman, turn to **323**.

255

The corridor turns sharply right again and you see a rough hole in the left-hand wall just big enough for you to climb through. You peer into the hole but can't really see much in the gloom beyond. Littlebig grabs a flaming torch from its holder on the wall and thrusts it through the hole to reveal a small cave that has been carved out of the rock. Its rough walls are covered with strange drawings and symbols. There are also some chains attached to the wall. If you want to climb through the hole into the cave, turn to **303**. If you would rather press on, turn to **108**.

256

The silver ball starts to warm up in your hand and is soon quite hot. It gets hotter and hotter until you cannot hold it any longer and are forced to drop it on the floor. In a blinding flash it explodes into tiny pieces that shoot out in all directions. *Test your Luck.* If you are Lucky, turn to **48**. If you are Unlucky, turn to **375**.

257

Whilst you are cutting through the cobwebs, a deadly black widow spider drops from the ceiling on to your back. *Test your Luck.* If you are Lucky, turn to **273**. If you are Unlucky, turn to **384**.

258

The mirror shatters and the terrible pain in your body slowly eases. When you finally recover you search the room but find nothing except a Gold Piece which is lodged in a crack in the floor. You decide to keep a piece of the mirror for LUCK and leave the room by the door opposite. Turn to **243**.

259

Littlebig kicks the door several times in frustration and hammers on it with his fists. Much to his surprise, a piece of paper suddenly appears from under the door. He picks it up and reads out a rhyme that is written on it:

> *'No key will open the iron door*
> *So ring a bell and count to four.'*

If you possess a brass bell, turn to **296**. If you do not have a bell, turn to **189**.

260

It is a very short rhyme that reads:

> *'Roses are red*
> *Violets are blue*
> *A face like yours*
> *Belongs in the zoo.'*

Without warning, twenty iron bars shoot up out of the sand and thump into the ceiling to trap you in the sand pit like a caged animal. The iron bars are too close together to allow you to squeeze out between them. If you have eaten green paste from a jar found in the green room, turn to **315**. If you have not eaten this paste, turn to **338**.

261

You sense that the dwarf you are fighting is not attacking with all his heart. You look into his eyes and see a look of desperation. It is the look of a friend who is fighting you against his will. You realize your mistake and turn to face the other dwarf. Turn to **97**.

262

As you walk along the corridor you step on a floor stone, which gives a little under your weight. You hear a click as an arrow is released from a hole in the wall. *Test your Luck.* If you are Lucky, the arrow misses you. If you are Unlucky, the arrow thuds into your leg. Lose 2 STAMINA points. Cursing loudly, you pull the arrow from your leg and limp up the corridor. Turn to **59**.

263

The Ghost lunges at you with its sword, as you run for the door, just catching you in the leg with the tip of the blade. Lose 2 STAMINA points. But it doesn't stop you and you run out of the room as Littlebig slams the door in the Ghost's face. 'Come on!' shouts Littlebig. 'Let's go!' Needing no encouragement, you hurry along the corridor. Turn to **94**.

264

As you walk towards the door, the wizard shouts out in an angry voice, 'Those who have no time to talk to me always pay a price!' There is a sudden flash of light and you are smashed to the ground by an invisible force. Lose 2 STAMINA points. When you stand up, your backpack feels a little lighter. Roll 1 die. This is the number of items you must lose to the wizard who has taken them into his dimension. You waste no more time and dash out of the room and up the corridor. Turn to **65**.

265

There is a new passageway in the right-hand wall that you see some forty metres ahead. A hooded figure wearing dark robes suddenly appears from around the corner carrying a black sack over his shoulder. In his right hand you see a long dagger. The figure sees you, stops and turns, and runs back the way he came. 'Hey! Come back!' Littlebig shouts. His cries echo down the corridor but the hooded figure does not return. You decide to run after it and turn right down the new corridor. Turn to **224**.

266

As you walk through the enormous cave you see what appears to be a large boulder some three metres high. But all of a sudden it moves. Standing before you on its huge trunk-like legs is a fearsome beast with the most terrifying head you have ever seen. Its skull is missing in parts, exposing sections of its pulsating red brain. It has many horns that grow out of the rest of its skull like spikes. Its teeth are long and sharp, its nose is flat and dripping, and its two eyes are tiny and close together. Its body is rock-like and its huge muscular arms end in massive stone fists. The GIGANTUS is delirious with hunger and is eager to rip you apart.

GIGANTUS   SKILL 12   STAMINA 12

The beast's prodigious strength will cause 4 STAMINA points of damage if it wins an Attack Round. But during each Attack Round you will have two attacks, one for yourself and one for Littlebig who has a SKILL of 8. However, the Gigantus will only attack you. If you win, turn to **133**.

267

Miraculously, the second fireball misses you by centimetres. It flies past your head before exploding against the wall at the end of the corridor. You rush in to attack the Wizard who is now forced to defend himself with a short sword that is made of an unusually dark metal.

EVIL WIZARD   SKILL 8   STAMINA 8

If you lose an Attack Round, turn to **81**. If you win without losing an Attack Round, turn to **113**.

268

'Some people never learn,' Vigdis says with a sigh. Her image suddenly grows in size. She reaches towards you and wraps you in her ghostly arms. You try to run away but are unable to move your legs. Your mind races and you start to panic. Vigdis meant what she said. She utters an arcane spell and your body slowly changes into that of a Vampire Bat. Vigdis is pleased that she has another pet, but for you the adventure is over.

269

Littlebig's face is frozen with fear as the dragon stirs. Its tail swishes from side to side and one giant eye flicks open to spy on the intruders. It sees you immediately and you have no choice but to fight the enraged beast.

BLACK DRAGON   SKILL 14   STAMINA 18

The dragon will concentrate its attack on you but you will have two strikes each Attack Round, one for yourself and one for Littlebig. During the first Attack Round you must *Test your Luck* to see if you are caught within the poisonous gas cloud that the dragon blows out at you. If you are Lucky, it misses. If you are Unlucky, lose 4 STAMINA points. If, somehow, you manage to defeat the mighty dragon, turn to **337**.

270

The cursed bracelet has some use after all. It counteracts the magic of the cursed sword that you are suddenly able to throw on the ground. If you have not done so already, you may either read the scroll (turn to **86**) or examine the painting (turn to **184**). If you would rather climb back down the rope and walk back down the corridor, turn to **144**.

271

For each Flesh Grub that is alive you must lose 1 STAMINA point. If you are still alive, roll two dice again to decide how many of the remaining Flesh Grubs you kill this time. If the number rolled is the same or greater than the number of Flesh Grubs, turn to 102. If the number rolled is less than the number of Flesh Grubs, turn to 63.

272

The bracelet shimmers slightly as you slide it over your wrist. It suddenly feels hot as it tightens around you, burning the skin. The bracelet is cursed by evil magic! Lose 1 SKILL point and 1 STAMINA point. Unable to remove it, you have no choice but to jump down into the room below. Turn to 64.

273

Fortunately for you, Littlebig is standing near and sees the spider land on you. He quickly flicks it off your back and stamps on it with his large boot. 'That would not have been funny,' says Littlebig, serious for once. 'Little insect, big bite!' Watching each other's back, you carry on your search of the room. Turn to 148.

274

As you tiptoe across the floor you step on a rat's skull that cracks under the weight of your boot. *Test your Luck*. If you are Lucky, turn to 23. If you are Unlucky, turn to 80.

275

You sense there is something not quite right about the old man and you keep your eye on him as you turn the corner. There is an unpleasant smell of sulphur in the air and that is usually the telltale sign of evil. You trust your instinct and turn around to attack the old man. Turn to **160**.

276

None of the keys that you have fit the rusty old padlock. One of them breaks off in the lock as you try to jam it in and becomes useless. Littlebig kicks the door several times in frustration before slumping on the floor cursing loudly. Suddenly, he goes quiet when he sees a piece of paper appear from under the door. He picks it up and reads out the rhyme that is written on it.

> *'No key will open the iron door*
> *So ring a bell and count to four.'*

If you have a brass bell, turn to **296**. If you do not possess a brass bell, turn to **189**.

277

The door opens into a small dungeon cell that is furnished with just a small wooden table on which a candle is burning. Rats scurry across the damp floor. At the back of the cell you see a short, stocky man chained to the wall. He has been stripped of his shirt and you see blood trickling down his side from a deep wound under his arm. He has pigtails and a long beard. His chin rests on his chest and he is moaning, obviously in some considerable pain. He must have heard you enter the room because he starts to speak slowly without looking up. 'I've told you a thousand times,' he croaks, 'I do not know where the emerald eye is. You might as well just kill me now and get it over and done with.' You feel terribly sorry for the poor dwarf, who thinks you are his jailor. You decide to help him, as he is probably a good-hearted treasure hunter like yourself. It doesn't take too long to free the dwarf who is both surprised and grateful to be rescued. You patch up his wounds as best you can and give him food and water. 'My name is Littlebig,' he says enthusiastically, 'I was ambushed five days ago by that evil, thieving, half-human called Sharcle. Have you ever heard of him? He comes from Saffrica. He would sell his own mother if he could get 2 Gold Pieces for her! But I'll get him one day and the world will be a better place for it.'

You decide to tell Littlebig about your quest and that you, too, are looking for the emerald eye. 'Well let's go and find it!' exclaims Littlebig. If Sharcle wants it so badly, it must be worth something!' You leave the cell and turn left up the corridor. 'Stop!' shouts Littlebig. 'There's a trap here.'

Littlebig drops to his knees and crawls slowly along the corridor, pressing down on all the floor stones. One of them gives way under the pressure and six darts immediately shoot out from narrow slits in both walls. They smash harmlessly into the opposite walls and Littlebig stands up with a smug grin on his face. 'Off we go!' he says in a jolly voice. You soon come to a junction in the corridor. If you want to turn left, turn to 354. If you want to turn right, turn to 202.

278

The leaf paste tastes disgusting and makes you feel quite sick. However, the feeling of nausea soon passes and is replaced by a feeling of strength and vitality. Add 1 SKILL point and 2 STAMINA points. At the bottom of the jar you are surprised to find a small silver key with the number 14 stamped on it. You put it in your pocket and leave the room. Turn to 142.

279

As you walk up to the old man, he leaps up into the air and instantly metamorphoses into a horrific beast, three metres high and covered in scaly black skin. Steam hisses from its nostrils and a terrible stench of sulphur belches out of its fanged mouth. It has a large, horned head and hands that end in hooked claws. It has cloven hooves and a long, vivid red tail. For a moment you are in shock as the HELL DEMON lashes out at you with its iron-like claws. Lose 4 STAMINA points. You reel back from the blow and hear Littlebig shouting something from behind you. You only catch two words '… wavy blade …' and they puzzle you. Suddenly the words make sense. If you have a kris knife, turn to **195**. If you do not have this knife, turn to **371**.

280

You close your hand slowly around the handle of the dagger and take a deep breath. 'You can do it!' Littlebig says encouragingly. You count to three and then pull on the handle as hard as you can. Despite pulling it with all your might, the dagger remains fixed in the wall. Turn to **38**.

281

Another door appears in the right-hand wall of the passageway. It is made of dark oak and is standing half open. If you want to enter the room, turn to **6**. If would rather keep on walking, turn to **112**.

282

Despite the darkness of the pit, you can see all the way to the bottom. The floor is totally covered by hundreds of large scorpions and bloated, hairy spiders crawling over each other. It's a trap and not an exit from the cavern. You call to Littlebig that you are coming back up.

'So what are we going to do now?' asks Littlebig. If you want to walk on, turn to **4**. If you would rather walk back to the staircase in the cavern wall, turn to **318**.

283

As you leave the room, you are hit on the head by an invisible club and are knocked to the ground by the force of the blow. Lose 1 STAMINA point. You scramble to your feet and leave the room before the angry wizard attacks you again. Turn to **65**.

284

When you reach the door, the voice calling to you falls silent. You turn the handle and enter a small room. A door in the opposite wall closes as you walk in the room. There is a table against the left-hand wall on which stand a bowl of steaming soup. A chair lies on its side on the floor by the table. Nailed to the wall above the table are many sheets of paper. Will you:

Read the sheets of paper?	Turn to **240**
Drink the soup?	Turn to **89**
Open the door opposite?	Turn to **312**

285

You hardly have time to draw breath before the other Uglukk Orc kicks the table away and charges at you wielding its club. You take a step back to defend yourself and stumble on a large bone on the floor. *Test your Luck.* If you are Lucky, turn to **313**. If you are Unlucky, turn to **28**.

286

You arrive at a wooden door in the left-hand wall that has the words 'Store Room' etched into it. The door is not locked and the handle turns easily. If you want to enter the Store Room, turn to **361**. If you would rather keep on walking, turn to **346**.

287

The pouch contains a tiny bottle made of purple frosted glass. The bottle has a glass stopper. It is impossible to tell if there is anything inside the bottle. If you want to remove the stopper, turn to **117**. If you would rather leave it and walk on, turn to **376**.

288

You soon arrive back at the junction. To your right you see the stairs leading back up to the woodcutter's hut. It suddenly becomes clear to you that this quest is going to be very difficult and you are tempted to climb the stairs. But you urge yourself on, convincing yourself that you will succeed. Turn to **88**.

289

You stand with your sword at the ready as Littlebig prises open the box. He peers inside and says in a moaning voice, 'All that effort just to find two pairs of old boots!' He hands one pair to you and you see that there is a shoemaker's mark that you recognize on the sole. You tell Littlebig with some satisfaction that these are Elven Boots that enable people who wear them to walk silently wherever they go. Without any hesitation you put them on. Add 1 SKILL point. Littlebig complains that he should not be wearing anything that has been made by an elf and puts them on reluctantly, muttering under his breath. Out of curiosity you decide to move the box away from the wall. Turn to **326**.

290

You walk no more than three paces before the sand starts to rise in a long line as though something is swimming just beneath the surface. Suddenly something breaks through the sand and rears in the air, ready to strike. Its body is long and bloated and divided into many segments like a gigantic maggot. Its head does not have eyes but powerful scent glands above its enormous mouth which is lined with spiked teeth. The GIANT SANDWORM has not eaten in four weeks and intends to feed on you. You must fight to save your life.

GIANT SANDWORM   SKILL 8   STAMINA 10

If you have a crystal blade dagger, turn to **367**. If you do not have this dagger you must defend yourself with your sword. If you win, turn to **47**.

You watch Littlebig whistling happily to himself, as
he walks along, and feel very pleased to have such a
good companion with you to explore this infernal
dungeon. Then a dark thought suddenly crosses your
mind. What if you do not find the emerald eye and
have to return to the Blue Pig Tavern empty handed
and explain to Henry Delacor that you have failed?
Would he believe you? Would he still give you the
antidote to the poison? You talk to Littlebig about
your concerns and he replies in his usual jovial way,
'Well, we are going to find the emerald eye and the
golden dragon, so failure is out of the question. And if
that Henry what's-his-name refuses to give you the
antidote, he will have me to deal with. Ha!' Littlebig's
optimism is infectious and you feel immediately posi-
tive again. Looking ahead to the junction at the end of
the corridor you see a scrawny, little old man with
a very long white beard sitting on a wooden chair
facing you. He doesn't seem particularly concerned at
seeing you. He slowly puffs out his cheeks and starts
humming a song to himself. Will you:

Attack him with your sword?	Turn to **160**
Talk to him?	Turn to **30**
Ignore him and turn left?	Turn to **363**
Ignore him and turn right?	Turn to **122**

292

The walls grind steadily towards each other as you gather your thoughts to remember the spell. But can you remember it exactly? Will you shout:

Agga Zagga Zoo?	Turn to **217**
Azang Bazang-zang?	Turn to **351**
Arr Booda Ba?	Turn to **402**

293

The door opens into a small room. As you walk in the door slams shut. Behind you stands an ugly, brown-skinned creature, about a metre and a half tall, who is dressed in animal skins. It is a GOBLIN armed with two daggers, intent on slaying you for your treasure.

GOBLIN   SKILL 5   STAMINA 5

If you win, turn to **146**.

294

As you raise your sword arm a bolt of lightning shoots out from the crystal and slams into your chest. Lose 1 SKILL point and 4 STAMINA points. Even if you are still alive you are dazed and confused and in some considerable pain. Littlebig tries to support you as Lo Lo Mai says angrily,

> *'Foolish warrior tell me how*
> *You think you will defeat me now*
> *One chance is all you have, no more,*
> *Ten Gold Pieces open yonder door.'*

If you want to attack her again, turn to **75**. If you have 10 Gold Pieces to pay her instead, turn to **110**.

295

The Niblicks' lair is a veritable treasure trove. You find some bread and apples in the sacks, which you eat very quickly. Add 2 STAMINA points. Next, you examine the armour and weapons and help yourself to a fine bronze shield. Add 1 SKILL point. Most of the swords are no better than your own, but a black sword with a large ruby set in the handle catches your eye. One of the chests contains a rolled up scroll. And one of the vases contains a copper key with the number 192 stamped on it. The only other thing of real interest is an old painting of a dragon. After placing the key in your pocket, you decide what to do. Will you:

Pick up the black sword?   Turn to **345**
Read the scroll?   Turn to **86**
Examine the painting?   Turn to **184**

296

You reach for the brass bell in your backpack and follow the instructions by ringing it four times. Much to your amazement the rusty lock unlocks itself and the iron door creaks open into a stone-walled corridor. Looking right, you see many broken bones strewn along the corridor floor. Looking left, you just catch sight of somebody running away and disappearing around a corner. If you want to look at the bones, turn to **253**. If you want to follow the person who ran away, turn to **92**.

297

As you place the necklace over your head you see two ghostly figures before your eyes. Two shimmering skeletons armed with swords seem to be coming right at you! It is as if they are running right through you and then they are gone. Everything appears to be normal again and, slightly shaken, you leave the room. Turn to **281**.

298

You grab hold of the spear with both hands and get ready to pull. 'Go on, you can do it!' says Littlebig excitedly. The spear comes out of the wall as though it had been lodged in butter rather than rock. You tumble backwards a couple of steps but remain on your feet. Littlebig cheers loudly, but now you must make your second choice. Will you:

Pull the sword?	Turn to **106**
Pull the dagger?	Turn to **280**
Pull the axe?	Turn to **321**
Pull the arrow?	Turn to **353**

299

You find nothing but maggots and lice in the Uglukk Orc's clothing and move over to the Mercenary. His pockets contain 2 Gold Pieces, a fish hook, a small brass bell and three copper buttons. After taking what you want, you decide what to do next. If you have not done so already, you may search the cavern (turn to **127**) or you may leave the cavern (turn to **76**).

300

'After you,' Littlebig says with a smile, while bowing in mock deference. You breathe in deeply and jump on to the first stepping stone. To your amazement nothing untoward happens to you. You jump between the stepping stones until you reach the flat corridor floor again. 'Wait for me!' Littlebig shouts, as he jumps awkwardly from stone to stone. Despite a couple of wobbly landings, he reaches you safely. Turn to **255**.

301

Walking along, you hear a new sound echoing through the cavern, like that of many groaning voices. From out of the gloom step six shuffling figures wearing tattered rags. Their pallid skin is scarred and peeling, and their vacant, hollow eyes stare blankly from their tortured-looking faces. Suddenly animated by your presence, the ZOMBIES lurch towards you with their clawed hands outstretched. If you have a Ring of Zombie control, turn to **58**. If you do not have this ring you can either fight the Zombies (turn to **310**) or try to run for it (turn to **78**).

302

Upon standing on the footmarks, the room appears to spin before your eyes. You lose your sense of balance and fall over feeling sick. You fall in and out of consciousness and lose track of time. When you come to, you stand up to find yourself in a different place. You are back in the woodcutter's hut with only your sword, shield and empty backpack. Everything that you had taken from the labyrinth is gone. You have been teleported back to the hut and must start your adventure again. But you are much weaker now. Lose 4 SKILL points and 4 STAMINA points. Turn to **69**.

303

As Littlebig gets close to the writing on the wall, he starts to chuckle to himself. 'I think this cave used to be an old prison cell,' Littlebig says. 'All these symbols are written in dwarf and poke fun at the Half-Orc captors of the poor soul who was held here. Some of them are quite funny. This one says, "Orcs are more stupid than forks." And this one says "The only good Orc is a dead Orc". I wonder what happened to the dwarf? Hello, what's this?' Littlebig crouches down and looks closely at some symbols inside a circle. 'It says here "Black Dragon leads to Gold Dragon." I wonder if that could be the golden dragon we are looking for?' he says excitedly. A search of the cave reveals nothing else of interest so you climb back out into the corridor and walk on. Turn to **108**.

304

The corridor soon turns sharply to the right. You arrive at a large, wooden door in the left-hand wall. You press your ear to the door and hear the sound of somebody eating very noisily. If you want to open the door, turn to **111**. If you would rather keep walking up the corridor, turn to **76**.

305

You manage to climb down to the cave floor without waking the giant dragon. Beyond the dragon you can see a much larger tunnel entrance. If you are wearing Elven Boots, turn to **194**. If you are not wearing these boots, turn to **335**.

306

You breathe in deeply and run up to the edge of the pit to jump as high and far as you can. Roll two dice. If the total is the same or less than your SKILL, turn to **190**. If the total is greater than your SKILL, turn to **55**.

307

Just metres beyond the door, one of the floor stones moves slightly as you step on it. Too late you notice the narrow slits in the walls on both sides of the corridor. You have sprung a trap and six darts shoot out at you. *Test your Luck*. If you are Lucky, turn to **77**. If you are Unlucky, turn to **174**.

308

You see that the symbol is a white star. You look left and right down the corridor and see that both ways end with doors. There is nobody to be seen, but suddenly you hear an eerie, whispering voice coming from the left saying 'Come this way' over and over again. Then you hear a shrill female voice coming from the right saying 'No' over and over again. If you want to go left, turn to **154**. If you want to go right, turn to **284**.

309

One of the Skeletons was wearing a helmet which is etched with mysterious runes. The helmet is made of heavy iron and you think it might have magical properties. If you want to wear it, turn to **121**. If you would rather walk on without it, turn to **134**.

310

The Zombies are slow and clumsy, and you are able to fight them one at a time. You decide to take on four of them, leaving two for Littlebig to take care of.

	SKILL	STAMINA
First ZOMBIE	6	6
Second ZOMBIE	6	7
Third ZOMBIE	5	7
Fourth ZOMBIE	5	5

If you win, turn to **178**.

311

You open drawers and look in cupboards, but find little more than broken crockery and general mess. You walk over to a pile of logs by the stove. Behind the logs you find a large axe with a broken handle. There is a strange inscription etched into the axe head that has no meaning to you. Intrigued, you put the axe head in your backpack hoping it may be of use to you later. You walk over to the trap door and walk down the stairs. Turn to **69**.

312

You enter another small room with a door in the wall opposite. Standing in the middle of the room is a small, eastern-looking girl with short dark hair and cat-like eyes. She is wearing a white silk robe. In her left hand she is holding two sheets of paper and in her right hand she is holding a triangular-shaped crystal. In a calm voice she says, 'Hello, my name is Lo Lo Mai. My words of wisdom tell no lie.' Will you:

Attack her with your sword?	Turn to **294**
Speak to her?	Turn to **249**
Walk past her and open the other door?	Turn to **396**

313

You regain your balance and ready yourself for the ferocious battle.

UGLUKK ORC   SKILL 8   STAMINA 9

If you are still alive after three Attack Rounds, turn to **161**.

314

Littlebig produces some old cheese, some stale biscuits and a leather flask of goat's milk. Though it was hardly tasty, you welcome the nourishment and even manage a thirty-minute nap. Add 2 STAMINA points. Feeling much better, you decide to follow the wall around the cavern. Turn to **40**.

315

There appears to be no way out of the cavern. As a last resort you pull on the iron bars and are amazed to see that they bend. The green paste has given you super strength and the ability to bend metal. With ease you pull two bars apart to enable you to escape. If you have not done so already, you may either open the wooden chest (turn to **327**) or strike the staff on the floor (turn to **198**). If you would rather leave the cavern and follow the arrows, turn to **248**.

316

As you leap sideways against the wall, you are caught by a glancing blow on the left shoulder from one of the ceiling stones. You feel a sharp pain that makes you cry out. Unfortunately you have fractured your collar bone. If you are carrying a shield, you will be unable to use it from now on and must leave it behind. Lose 2 STAMINA points. Littlebig tears a strip of cloth off the bottom of his tunic and makes a sling for your arm. Cursing your luck, you walk on. Turn to **255**.

Ahead you see that the corridor le
bridge which spans a deep pit. A r
the bridge descends into the dark
below. If you want to walk over th
on up the corridor, turn to **193**. If
climbing down the rope ladder, turn to **362**.

The steps that are cut into the wall of the cavern are very narrow and you have to concentrate so as not to fall. At last you reach the top of the steps and the relative safety of the alcove. There is an iron door at the back of the alcove that is firmly locked by a large padlock. If you possess a picklock, turn to **344**. If you do not have a picklock, turn to **159**.

There is nothing else of interest in the cave apart from the leather bag that contains a dagger, and a gold ring which fits nicely on the thumb of your left hand. You leave the cave and carry on up the corridor. Turn to **139**.

Littlebig is still without a weapon, so you must fight the Wizard on your own. As you close in on him he releases another fireball. Roll two dice. If the number rolled is less than or equal to your SKILL score, turn to **267**. If the number rolled is greater than your SKILL, turn to **216**.

321

You wrap both hands around the axe handle and breathe in deeply. 'Give it your best!' Littlebig says enthusiastically. Putting one leg against the wall to get better leverage, you pull the handle as hard as you can. Unfortunately, it does not move even a millimetre. Turn to **38**.

322

The door opens back on to a passageway and after walking along it for a few minutes you see another door in the left-hand wall. There is a small window in the door that looks into a candlelit room in which a woman sits at a bench with her back to you. You knock on the door but she does not stand up. If you want to enter the room, turn to **158**. If you wish to continue walking up the corridor, turn to **281**.

323

You arrive at the entrance to a cave in the right-hand wall of the corridor. Peering in, you see a stone table and four chairs. A burning candle housed in a large skull is giving off a dim and eerie light. Asleep in one of the chairs, and snoring loudly, you see the large bulk of an Ogre. It must be at least two metres tall. Its lumpy face is green and its open mouth is drooling spittle down its hairy chin. It is wearing animal skins and has a strange necklace made out of rats' skulls. A large wooden club leans against the chair, on the back of which hangs an old leather bag. If you want to creep into the room to take the bag, turn to **274**. If you want to carry on walking up the corridor, turn to **139**.

324

Half expecting something terrible to happen, you grimace as you slide the cord over your head. But nothing does happen, and you look around to see Littlebig still staring at the glass ball. If you want to let him touch it with his dagger, turn to **386**. If you want to leave the cellars and return to the corridor above, turn to **355**.

325

The gold key turns the lock of the gold box. It clicks open and inside you find a polished stone etched with the words 'five dagger'. Turn to **227**.

326

With Littlebig's help, you move the heavy box aside to reveal a hole in the wall no more than a metre in diameter. 'A tunnel!' shouts Littlebig excitedly. 'A secret tunnel! Come on, let's crawl through it.' If you want to crawl through the tunnel, turn to **405**. If you would rather throw a stone down the tunnel first, turn to **31**.

327

You lift the chest out of the sand pit and see that the iron hinges and lock are very rusty. One blow with your sword sends the lock flying through the air. Wary of traps, you lift the lid slowly and see a pile of Gold Pieces. You count 27 in total. If you have not done so already, you may either open the book (turn to **165**) or strike the staff on the floor (turn to **198**). Alternatively you may follow the arrows further (turn to **248**).

328

Although there is less than a thimble-full of liquid in the bottle, it is actually enough poison to kill twenty men. It is very quick acting and you fall over unconscious within seconds of drinking it. There is nothing Littlebig can do to save you. Your adventure is over.

TODAY'S SPECIALS

Chalk 1 Gold Piece
Garlic 1 Gold Piece
Silver Dagger 3 Gold Pieces
Carved Wooden Duck 2 Gold Pieces
Pickled Pigs' Tails 1 Gold Piece
Skunk Oil 2 Gold Pieces
Wax Candle 1 Gold Piece
Fish Hook 1 Gold Piece
Tin Whistle 1 Gold Piece
Dried .... Gold P...

329

The door opens into a small storeroom that is lined with shelves from floor to ceiling. The shelves are crammed with tins, boxes, jars, bottles, pots and objects of all shapes and sizes. Behind the counter at the back of the room stands an old man wearing a white apron. He bids you good day in a friendly voice and reaches down to produce a small chalkboard on which is written:

Today's Specials

Chalk:	1 Gold Piece
Garlic:	1 Gold Piece
Silver Dagger:	3 Gold Pieces
Carved Wooden Duck:	2 Gold Pieces
Pickled Pigs' Tails:	1 Gold Piece
Skunk Oil:	2 Gold Pieces
Wax Candle:	1 Gold Piece
Fish Hook:	1 Gold Piece
Tin Whistle:	1 Gold Piece
Dried Mushrooms:	1 Gold Piece

If you wish to buy any of the items, you must pay the merchant in gold before leaving the room. Turn to **262**.

330

Ahead in the corridor, you see the skeletal figure of a fallen warrior lying face down on the stone floor. He still clutches his sword in his skeletal hand and his body has leather armour over a purple tunic. A leather bag is strapped to his belt and there is a small silver flask around his neck on a silver chain. If you want to take a closer look at the items, turn to **143**. If you would rather keep on walking, turn to **212**.

331

Luckily for you, the snake's head necklace is a magic charm, which counters the evil magic of the helmet. Add 1 LUCK point. Now instead of draining your life, the helmet will help defend you in combat. Add 1 SKILL point. Leaving the Skeletons behind, you walk on down the corridor. Turn to **134**.

332

You have drunk the same strong poison that killed the warrior. The only difference is that he was forced to drink it by an evil wizard, whereas you drank it of your own accord! The result, however, is the same. You sink to your knees, clutching your stomach, as Littlebig watches on in horror. You slump forward and lose consciousness, and in less than a minute it's all over. Your adventure ends here.

333

Gripping the staff tightly, you strike its end as hard as you can against the floor.

'Hold on to me tightly Littlebig,' you shout at the top of your voice. There is an almighty, deafening crack of thunder, followed by a massive shock wave that rolls down the corridor like a giant invisible wave. Anything in its path is picked up and rolled along at high speed, including the evil wizard who attacked you. Moments later all is quiet again and the wizard is nowhere to be seen. 'That will teach him to attack a couple of adventurers who meant him no harm,' mutters Littlebig. 'Come on, let's get going,' you say, slapping him on the back. 'There is no time to lose!' Turn to **291**.

334

You tell the Mercenary that you will pay him to help you. Swinging his mighty two-handed sword through the air, the Mercenary strides towards the Uglukk Orc, which is oblivious to the danger behind it. You watch the long blade rise and then fall heavily on the Orc's neck. For a moment its face shows a surprised look, as the Mercenary's blow strikes home. Then its mouth opens as if to scream, but all that comes out is the blood-gurgling sound of its dying howl. The Mercenary grunts in satisfaction and holds out his huge hand to demand payment. If you have 10 Gold Pieces and want to pay him, turn to **379**. If you do not have 10 Gold Pieces or you decide not to pay him, turn to **223**.

335

As you walk around the slumbering beast, Littlebig inadvertently kicks a loose stone across the floor. The noise echoes noisily around the cave. *Test your Luck.* If you are Lucky, turn to **203**. If you are Unlucky, turn to **269**.

336

You soon arrive at a formidable-looking iron door in the left-hand wall. If you want to try to open the door, turn to **293**. If you would rather walk on, turn to **173**.

337

Littlebig starts to complain that there is no treasure to be found in the dragon's lair. 'I mean, after all, dragons are supposed to guard huge hoards of treasure in their lairs aren't they? It's just not fair!' While half listening to his latest complaint, you look around the cave and see a new tunnel entrance that is much larger than the one from which you emerged. You tell Littlebig not to give up hope and start walking towards the new tunnel. Turn to **378**.

338

There appears to be no way out of the cavern. You pull on the iron bars with all your might but your efforts are futile. There is no way out. You realize that you will perish when your food and water eventually run out, or when the poison that you took in the Blue Pig Tavern has its full effect on you. Your adventure ends here.

339

As you attempt to swerve around the Zombie you stumble over a rock and fall over. The Zombies move in to surround you and you have no option but to fight them. Turn to **310**.

340

You question your own wisdom to drink water that is coming from the mouth of such an ugly old crone, but your hunch is right. The water is pure and has magical properties. Add 2 STAMINA points. With renewed energy you walk up the corridor. Turn to **136**.

341

You stagger back from the force of the blow and receive another terrible blast on the back of the head from the warhammer of the second Littlebig. You drop to the floor semi-conscious and see both dwarves standing over you. One of them starts to metamorphose before your very eyes. It turns into a hideous-looking creature, some two metres tall with scarlet scales and an oversized, pulsating skull. Its eyes are large and red-veined, and its mouth is small with long, protruding lips. Despite your blurred vision there is no mistaking a Doppelgänger. You realize that you made a mistake and attacked your dwarf friend. As you lose consciousness you see the Doppelgänger strike Littlebig who is powerless against its mind control. Your adventure is over.

342

You sense something strange about the old man and watch him carefully as you turn the corner to walk past. Although you did not know it, the armband used to belong to a powerful cleric who spent his time ridding the world of demons. Had the armband not protected you, the little old man might not have been as harmless as he appeared. You hurry on until the old man is out of sight. Turn to **286**.

343

As you enter the room, you hear a rustling noise and see some of the leaves move. You draw your sword and prepare yourself for combat. Suddenly a small, sinewy, green GREMLIN jumps out in front of you brandishing a short sword. He is bare-chested and is only wearing a loin cloth. He crouches down and then leaps high into the air straight at you, screaming at the top of his scratchy voice.

GREMLIN   SKILL 4   STAMINA 3

If you defeat the nasty little creature, turn to **395**.

344

You set to work trying to open the rusty padlock with the picklock. Although you do not possess the skills of a thief, you manage to open the lock in less than five minutes. Littlebig is very impressed. You push on the iron door and it opens out into a stone-walled corridor. Looking right, you see many broken bones strewn along the corridor floor. Looking left, you just catch sight of somebody running away and disappearing around a corner. If you want to examine the bones, turn to **253**. If you want to follow the person who ran away, turn to **92**.

345

The sword was made hundreds of years ago for an evil necromancer by the name of Razaak. It is a cursed sword and can only be used by evil wizards who have the power to control it. As soon as you touch the handle of the sword, it starts to move of its own accord. Even though you are holding on tightly to the handle, the blade starts to move towards your throat! Beads of sweat roll down your forehead as you strain to keep the tip of the sword from piercing your flesh. If you are wearing a gold bracelet, turn to **270**. If you do not have this item, turn to **93**.

346

As you walk further along the corridor, you notice that the temperature drops significantly. The walls on both sides are wet and there is a strong acid-like smell in the air. In the distance you see that the passageway turns sharply left. Littlebig runs ahead and carefully peers around the corner. 'I can't see very far,' he whispers, 'it's so misty. Maybe we should go back the other way?' If you want to go back, turn to **237**. If you would rather walk on into the mist, turn to **126**.

347

You reach into your backpack and pull out the orb. The moment you touch it, gentle music starts to play. It has an immediate effect on the Ghost, which stops in its tracks and slowly starts to fade from view. Its sword clatters to the floor and seconds later the Ghost has disappeared. Littlebig looks very relieved. Although uninjured, apart from a nick on his forearm, he is bathed in sweat from the exertion of combat. 'You search the room,' he says in short breaths, 'I need a rest'. You examine all the swords and find one of the best you have ever seen in your life. You take it and leave your own behind. Add 1 SKILL point. Happy with your new weapon, you leave the room and walk on. Turn to **94**.

348

As you lunge at the old man with your sword, the painting's canvas tears and from it leaps a HOWLING WOLF. Sharp teeth protrude from its slavering mouth. The old man calls the wolf to rip the flesh from your bones.

HOWLING WOLF   SKILL 7   STAMINA 8

If you win, turn to **218**.

349

Littlebig does all he can to revive you with herbs and potions that he brought with him from his village. Eventually the fever subsides and, although weak, you feel well enough to continue your quest. Lose 1 SKILL point and turn to **148**.

350

When you pull on the rope you hear the sound of a bell ring. It is not very loud, but loud enough to alert anybody above of your presence. Looking up at the hole in the ceiling you think you could just about squeeze yourself through it if you were to climb up the rope. If this is what you want to do, turn to **8**. If you would rather walk back down the corridor, turn to **144**.

351

As you shout the words there is a blinding flash of light. What looks like a shimmering ball of white light flies from your fingertips and smashes into the wall opposite the iron door. A hole about a metre in diameter appears as the two other walls grind steadily towards each other. You are about to jump through the hole in the wall when Littlebig calls for you to wait. 'Look!' he shouts. 'There's a large emerald lying in the shards of broken glass!' If you want to pick up the emerald, turn to **7**. If you would rather not waste any more time and jump through the hole in the wall, turn to **183**.

352

If you have a potion of healing in your backpack, turn to **17**. If you do not have this potion, turn to **115**.

353

You take hold of the arrow with both hands and give it a sharp tug. Much to your relief, it comes out of the wall as easily as the spear. Littlebig lets out another loud cheer and says, 'Come on, only three to go!' But which weapon will be your third choice? Will you:

Pull the sword?   Turn to **18**
Pull the dagger?   Turn to **251**
Pull the axe?   Turn to **214**

354

The dimly lit passageway stretches into the distance as far as you can see. The walls and floor are damp and there is a musty smell in the air. Littlebig seems unconcerned by the situation and starts talking loudly, his words echoing down the passage. 'I don't suppose you ever met my famous uncle Bigleg did you?' he asks excitedly. Without waiting for an answer he says, 'Bigleg died a hero saving the dwarves of Stonebridge! That's the village where I come from too. It's just north of where we are now in Darkwood Forest or, as some folk call it, the Forest of Doom. Bigleg was a good friend of Yaztromo, the most famous wizard in Allansia. Now you must have heard of him! Anyway …'. Littlebig stops talking mid-sentence when you see something on fire flying down the corridor towards you at high speed. It's a fireball and it's coming straight at you. 'Look out!' screams Littlebig, pushing you against the wall. The fireball flies past you and you watch it explode at the end of the passage. 'Missed! I can't believe it!' shouts a man in a gruff voice. You look ahead again to see a man in purple robes appear out of the smoke with his arms pointing at you. He is bald and wears a pointed purple skullcap. His short beard is also pointed and he looks very angry. He starts to mutter an incantation, readying himself to cast another spell. You are being attacked by an EVIL WIZARD. Will you:

Attack him with your sword?	Turn to **320**
Use one of your magic items?	Turn to **177**
Offer him some gold pieces?	Turn to **96**

355

You soon arrive at an oak door in the right-hand wall. You press your ear against the door and hear the sound of metal clashing against metal: possibly the sound of a sword fight. If you want to open the door, turn to **42**. If you would rather keep walking, turn to **238**.

356

You have only gone a few metres when you run, literally, into a shower of Death Slime as it senses your presence. It is impossible to avoid being hit by the acid jelly and you scream out in pain as it burns through your skin. There is no escape and you suffer a painful and unpleasant end. Your adventure is over.

357

You reach out to take the emerald but grab nothing but air. The jewel is an illusion! The cauldron suddenly explodes, sending shards of pot and boiling sludge flying everywhere. Roll 1 die and reduce your STAMINA by the number rolled. If you are still alive, turn to **226**.

358

The sword is finely crafted and is made of the finest steel that you have ever seen in your life. There is an inscription running down the centre of the blade which reads 'Have no fear, skullsplitter is here.' 'That's encouraging,' says Littlebig, 'I prefer a war-hammer myself, but go ahead and take it. Enjoy yourself!' The skullsplitter sword will definitely aid you in combat. Add 1 SKILL point. If you have not done so already, you may either open the leather bag (turn to 114) or uncork the silver flask (turn to 245). The only other option you have is to walk on (turn to 212).

359

The angry Troll walks slowly towards you swinging its mighty axe through the air. You breathe in deeply and charge at the Troll.

TWO-HEADED TROLL   SKILL 8   STAMINA 9

If you win, turn to 43.

360

Unsure as to whether the dwarf you are about to fight is your friend or a Doppelgänger, you wield your sword more in defence than attack.

LITTLEBIG   SKILL 8   STAMINA 10

If you win the first Attack Round, turn to 261. If you lose the first Attack Round, turn to 341.

361

The room is quite small and crammed with casks, barrels, boxes, vases, tins, sacks, jars, bottles and pots. There is quite a bad smell in the room. Littlebig starts opening some of the jars and tins, and prises the lids off some of the barrels. 'Ugh!' he says grimly, 'Everything is rotten. All this stuff must have been dumped in here years ago. The maggots and cockroaches must love it in here! Shall we go?' If you want to leave the storeroom and press on, turn to **346**. If you would rather continue your search of the room, turn to **36**.

362

It takes quite a long time to reach the bottom of the pit. It is almost pitch black and you can hardly see anything at all. As your eyes adjust to the gloom you hear some shuffling sounds coming from in front of you. Slowly, a vile undead creature lumbers towards you. Its decaying innards protrude through holes in its maggot-ridden flesh. Its swollen tongue hangs down from its sickly purple mouth and its deep-sunken red eyes stare straight at you. Gurgling and hissing, the GHOUL steps forward to attack.

GHOUL   SKILL 8   STAMINA 7

If the Ghoul manages to hit you four times, you will be paralysed and eaten later. If you win, turn to **155**.

363

If you are wearing a silver armband, turn to **91**. If you are not wearing a silver armband, turn to **275**.

364

You find a dirty old sack jammed into a crevice in the wall of the cavern. You open it and find a large gold coin inside that has a dragon's head stamped on one side and an eye on the other side. 'That's encouraging,' says Littlebig excitedly. 'We must be getting close to our goal now.' You place the coin in your pocket and walk over to the new tunnel. Turn to 233.

365

As soon as the door shuts behind you, you hear the sound of metal grating against stone. Suddenly, the floor opens up beneath your feet and the corridor section you are standing on collapses. You slide feet first down a dark stone chute and are unable to stop yourself from falling to the bottom. *Test your Luck*. If you are Lucky, turn to 105. If you are Unlucky, turn to 179.

366

It takes the strength of both of you to be able to pull the lever down and, as you do so, ten floor stones in the corridor ahead slowly rise up to look like a crooked line of stepping stones.

'Now do we walk along the top of the stones or avoid them like the plague?' asks Littlebig.

If you want to walk along the top of the stepping stones, turn to 300. If you want to walk along the corridor floor, turn to 44.

367

A voice in your head tells you to use the magic dagger instead of your sword. You obey the voice and stab the Sandworm as it lunges at you. The moment you strike the Sandworm stops, as though frozen in time. You watch on amazed as the stricken worm starts to crumble into grains of sand. In less than a minute the metamorphosis is complete. Turn to **47**.

368

Ten minutes later Littlebig gets very excited when he sees two symbols scratched on the left-hand wall. 'Secret door!' he says proudly. 'That's what it says. A secret door right here! Watch this.' He taps the symbols with his fingertips and suddenly a door appears in the wall. It opens by itself into a room that looks well equipped for comfort. There are chairs and a table, two beds, shelves piled high with food, water, books and even sheepskin rugs to cover the stone floor. 'It's a secret dwarf den,' Littlebig says proudly. 'It was built so that dwarves in danger could hide and rest. I haven't seen this one before. I don't know about you but I am tired and very hungry. It must be getting late and I could do with a good sleep.' If you want to sleep in the dwarf den, turn to **123**. If you would rather keep on walking, turn to **330**.

369

As you lower your hand into the pool, you feel a terrible burning sensation. The water in the pool contains transparent flesh-eating jellies to protect the coins. Lose 2 STAMINA points. You pull your hand out quickly and run to the door opposite. Turn to 322.

370

You react quickly and brush the rat off your leg before it can bite you. Littlebig stamps on it with his large boot, saying, 'You are lucky because that was a Fang Rat and they are deadly poisonous.' Then with a worried look he says, 'Do you know what? It's just my gut feeling, but I think we are going the wrong way. I think we should go the way that person did a few minutes ago.' You decide to take Littlebig's advice and go back to the corner where the figure disappeared. Turn to 206.

371

You shout back at Littlebig, above the screaming roar of the Hell Demon, telling him that you do not have a kris knife. 'Well, we are going to have to run for it as we have no hope of defeating a demon with normal weapons,' Littlebig shouts at the top of his voice. 'Quick, run!'

If you want to run down the left-hand corridor, turn to **208**. If you want to run down the right-hand corridor, turn to **180**.

372

The Vampire immediately stops in her tracks when she sees the garlic brandished in your hand. But this will only stop her for a few moments and you must decide quickly what to do next. If you wish to leave the room immediately, turn to **116**. If you have a silver dagger, turn to **163**. If you want to attack the Vampire with your sword, turn to **107**.

373

When you walk into the room, you have a weird feeling that all the people in the portraits are watching you. 'I'm sure the eyes are moving in some of these paintings,' whispers Littlebig. 'I think we should get out of here.' Will you:

Walk over to the large portrait?	Turn to **407**
Leave the room and walk on?	Turn to **70**
Go back to the door with the green square?	Turn to **141**

374

Much to your surprise, the door opens into a small room that is completely empty. As you step inside, the door closes behind you and the laughter stops. From nowhere, an old man's deep voice calmly says, 'Welcome friend'. If you wish to stay in the room, turn to **153**. If you would rather leave the room quickly and press on, turn to **283**.

375

You are hit in the leg by one of the flying shards of metal. Lose 2 STAMINA points. Littlebig helps you to bandage the wound and can't resist saying 'I told you so'. In some considerable pain, you limp out of the storeroom and tell Littlebig that you will listen to him next time. Turn to **346**.

376

You reach the far side of the cavern where you see a staircase that has been roughly cut into the wall rise up some twenty metres to an alcove. 'Looks like this could be our only way out of here,' says Littlebig looking up. If you want to climb the staircase, turn to **318**. If you would rather look for another way out of the cavern, turn to **219**.

377

As your skin tightens and your muscles harden, you realize there is no hope of survival. The Medusa has turned you to stone. Your adventure ends here.

378

The tunnel is lit by flaming torches and is wide enough for you to be able to walk along side-by-side. Although the tunnel runs as straight as an arrow, there is a steady incline that makes the walk quite hard work. After fifteen minutes you come to a dead end where a smooth stone wall blocks the tunnel. Curiously, five weapons are sticking out of the wall – a sword, a dagger, an axe, a spear and an arrow. There are also five small square metal boxes set in the wall with a keyhole in each one. The doors are no more than 10 cm square and each is made of a different metal – silver, iron, bronze, gold and copper. There is a rolled up parchment on a wooden shelf nearby on the tunnel wall that Littlebig picks up. 'Look, there is a dragon in gold leaf on this parchment and some instructions written underneath,' he says excitedly. 'It says there is a treasure chamber on the other side of this sliding wall that is locked by magic. To open it, we have to pull the weapons out of the wall one by one in the correct order. The correct order can be found inside the five metal boxes that can only be opened by five magic keys of the same metal as the box. That's it. Sounds simple enough.' If you have some keys, turn to **175**. If you do not have any keys, turn to **390**.

379

You count out 10 Gold Pieces one by one and give them to the Mercenary. He stares at you coldly, grunts once and turns to walk out of the cavern. You decide to poke around the debris on the floor and find 2 Gold Pieces, a silver armband and a dark blue bottle with a cork in it. The rotten smell in the cavern is unbearable and you must decide what to do. If you want to uncork the bottle, turn to 24. If you want to leave the stinking cavern immediately, turn to 76.

380

The hideous beast slumps forward and lands face first in a shallow pool of its own disgusting slime. All the insects and worms start to jump or crawl off its body as it starts to shrivel, hissing and steaming, until it dissolves into a sticky mound of black jelly. An acrid, ammonia-like smell from the steam rising from the jelly fills your nostrils. 'This is the most disgusting stink I have ever smelt in my life,' says Littlebig, holding his nose. 'Let's go before our lungs collapse!' If you want to leave the cellar and continue your quest, turn to 355. If you would rather search the cellar, turn to 230.

381

The room is empty except for the sparkling object, which you see is a crystal pendant mounted on a silver chain. If you want to put it around your neck, turn to 239. If you would rather leave the room without the pendant and walk back down the corridor, turn to 365.

As the second thief falls to the floor, you see that Littlebig is locked in combat with the first hooded figure who came back to rob you. His hood has fallen back off his head to reveal the face of a man with a deep scar running from his eyebrow to his chin and an eye patch over his right eye. He wields his two daggers deftly, cutting and thrusting at Littlebig. But the noble dwarf stands his ground and defeats the thief with a heavy blow to the side of his head. All three of the thieves own swag bags and their contents add up to 7 Gold Pieces, a picklock, a silver cross, a silver pin and two fish hooks. 'Not much of a haul from three thieves,' Littlebig says. 'But these daggers are worth having. I was thinking that the one I was fighting was going to turn out to be Sharcle, but it wasn't him. I'd know that evil no-gooder if I saw him again. But there's still plenty of time to get even with him. What goes around comes around!' After taking the things you want, you set off again. Turn to **368**.

383

As you look at the cat, its eyes start to sparkle brightly. You become mesmerized by the sparkling eyes and are unable to look away. A terrible pain grips your head. It becomes so unbearable that you pass out. Lose 2 STAMINA points. When you wake some time later you see that the cat has completely turned to dust. Nursing a thumping headache, you leave the room. Turn to 204.

384

The spider crawls up your back on to your neck and, before you realize that it is there, it sinks its fangs into your skin. You cry out in pain and grab your neck, but there is nothing you can do to stop the poison from surging through your veins. If you have a Potion of Healing, turn to 168. If you do not have this potion, turn to 221.

385

Your energy continues to drain out of you. As you try to walk on down the corridor, you fall forward and land flat on your face on the cold stone floor. The helmet has you completely under its evil control. Your eyes flutter for a moment as everything around you fades into darkness. Soon your last breath is gone. Your adventure is over.

386

Littlebig barely taps the glass ball with the tip of his dagger, but it is enough to set off a magic trap! The ball cracks open and the old iron door slams shut with a loud bang. You hear an unnerving grating sound and realize with horror that two of the walls are slowly closing in on you. Littlebig runs over to the door but is unable to open it. 'It's locked! We are going to be crushed to death. What are we going to do?' Littlebig cries with fear in his voice. There appears to be no other means of escape. Only magic can save you now. If you know the 'Hole in the Wall' spell, turn to **292**. If you do not know this spell, turn to **130**.

387

You follow the arrows around a left-hand bend in the corridor until you reach another junction. The arrows lead down the corridor to your right. Looking to your left you see that the corridor ends at a cavern with a sunken floor that is full of sand. Several objects are sticking out of the sand but it is hard to tell what they are. There is a shovel lying on the sand in the centre of the pit. If you want to grab the shovel and dig out the objects from the sand, turn to **290**. If you would rather follow the arrows, turn to **248**.

388

Hanging on to the writhing snake with one hand, you attempt to hack off its tail as it darts in and out trying to coil itself around you. Roll two dice. If the number rolled is the same or less than your SKILL score, turn to **125**. If the number rolled is greater than your SKILL score, turn to **22**.

389

You take a step back before charging at the door. Roll two dice. If the total is the same or less than your SKILL, the door flies open (turn to **26**). If the total is greater than your SKILL, the door does not give way and all you succeed in doing is injuring your shoulder. Lose 1 STAMINA point. You may try again if you wish or you may choose to return to the junction in the corridor (turn to **88**).

390

Knowing that you are about to pull one of the weapons from the wall, Littlebig walks up to you and gives you two slaps on the back in encouragement. 'Good luck,' he says solemnly. 'I'm sure you'll choose the right one.' Will you:

Pull the sword?	Turn to **106**
Pull the dagger?	Turn to **280**
Pull the axe?	Turn to **321**
Pull the spear?	Turn to **298**
Pull the arrow?	Turn to **157**

391

The dragon drops on to the stone floor with a dull thump. It begins to lose its three-dimensional shape and is soon nothing more than a red stain on the floor. If you have not done so already, you may either pick up the black sword (turn to **345**) or read the scroll (turn to **86**). If you would rather climb back down the rope and walk back down the corridor, turn to **144**.

392

The deadly spider's fangs puncture the skin on the back of your hand. Its poison is powerful and takes effect quickly. Lose 1 SKILL point and 4 STAMINA points. If you are still alive, turn to **228**.

393

You enter a small room that is brightly lit by many burning candles, which have been stuck on top of just about every available flat surface. There are two glass tables with mirrored tops on which stand twenty or so bottles with wax-sealed corks and handwritten labels. Standing between the two tables is one of the most beautiful girls you have ever seen in your life. She is wearing black baggy silk pants and a short white top. Her bare shoulders are draped by long blonde hair. A large sparkling diamond covers her navel and she wears another one around her neck on a gold chain. A small bottle rests on the open palm of her left hand. She stares at you instantly with her ice-blue eyes while showing just the slightest hint of a smile, and says in a soft voice, 'If you need a cure, my potions are pure.' She then motions for you to drink from the bottle in her hand. Will you:

Drink from the bottle?	Turn to 11
Attack her with your sword?	Turn to 244
Politely refuse her offer and leave the room?	Turn to 265

394

You step on the ladder and start your descent. If you have recently drunk the water in the cavern pool, turn to 282. If you have not drunk this water, turn to 135.

395

Hidden by the plants at the back of the room, you find a wooden cupboard fixed to the wall. It is also painted green. You open the cupboard and see a small jar on the shelf. The jar contains a green paste that smells as bad as the plants, and you assume the paste is made of crushed leaves. If you want to eat some of the leaf paste, turn to **278**. If you would rather leave the room and continue walking up the corridor, turn to **142**.

396

Lo Lo Mai stares at you intensely as you walk past her. The door opens into a corridor that goes straight on for as far as you can see. You soon come to two doors next to each other in the left-hand wall. The first door has a green square painted on it and the next one has a blue triangle painted on it. Will you:

Open the door with the green square?	Turn to **141**
Open the door with the blue triangle?	Turn to **53**
Keep on walking along the corridor?	Turn to **70**

397

Holding the shield firmly in front of you, you crouch down behind it as the fireball hits. Only your hand is burned where it is holding the red-hot shield. Lose 1 STAMINA point. You stand up quickly and attack the Wizard, who is now forced to defend himself with a short sword made of an unusually dark metal.

EVIL WIZARD   SKILL 8   STAMINA 8

If you lose an Attack Round, turn to **81**. If you win without losing an Attack Round, turn to **113**.

398

You pass the oak door, the stone throne and the fountain, and finally arrive at the junction. Ignoring the passageway to the left, up which you walked, you press on. Turn to **54**.

399

You step over the broken bones of the Skeleton King and look inside the coffin. There is a lot of dirt and debris but also something that looks very interesting. It is a golden orb that has two bands of diamond-shaped pieces of mother of pearl running around it. If you want to pick up the orb, turn to **205**. If you would rather leave it where it is and walk on, turn to **156**.

Clutching at a deep wound in his stomach, Sharcle drops to his knees and pleads for mercy. You ignore him and tend to Littlebig, who is still alive, but has lost a lot of blood. You see Sharcle's leather bag on the ground and find a bottle inside with the words 'Healing Potion' written on a label. 'Give it to me,' pleads Sharcle.

'Drink … it … yourself,' whispers Littlebig to you. There is less than a teaspoonful left in the bottle but you have no doubt who is going to drink it. You press the bottle to Littlebig's lips and tell him to drink. One gulp is enough and the potion is gone. In less than ten minutes Littlebig is up on his feet and fully recovered. Sharcle, meanwhile, is now slumped over and silent. Littlebig presses his ear against Sharcle's chest to listen to his breathing. 'Nothing. He's had it. He's a dead dog. But let's not cry over that. Come on my friend, I've got to get you to Stonebridge. We have some powerful healers there who can deal with most poisons.' Two days later, you are welcomed by the dwarf villagers of Stonebridge. The whole village is celebrating King Gillibran's birthday. Joining him in his celebrations is the Grand Wizard of Yore, Yaztromo, who has made a rare visit. News of your quest spreads quickly through the village and you are invited with Littlebig to join Yaztromo and the King at his table for a feast. Littlebig recounts the whole adventure in great detail and asks Yaztromo if he has any antidotes for slow-acting poison. Yaztromo looks at you and says slowly in a deep voice, 'Poisoned?

You're not poisoned. If you had drunk slow-acting poison you would be near death by now. That was just another of Sharcle's lies to make sure you came back to him. Forget about it and enjoy yourself.' With good friends and a golden dragon worth more than you could ever have imagined, it would be difficult not to enjoy yourself. And so you do.

401

You just manage to run out of the room and slam the door in the Ghost's face. 'Come on!' shouts Littlebig, 'Let's go!' Needing no encouragement, you hurry along the corridor. Turn to 94.

402

You recite the magic spell as loud as you can, but to your horror the walls carry on grinding towards each other. Turn to 130.

403

As you run past the Skeletons, they both take a swipe at you with their swords. *Test your Luck*. If you are Lucky, turn to 246. If you are Unlucky, turn to 207.

404

You try charging down the door together, but all you manage to do is to injure your shoulder. Lose 1 STAMINA point. You finally give up and walk to the corner where you saw the figure disappear. Turn to 206.

405

Littlebig sighs and says, 'I suppose I had better go first, seeing as I am smaller than you.' You watch him disappear into the dark tunnel on his hands and knees, and follow him after a few moments. Two minutes later, Littlebig calls back to tell you that he has come to the end of the tunnel and that it leads into a cavern. Then you hear him scream. You crawl as fast as you can until you reach the end of the tunnel. Without stopping, you stand up and find yourself in a small cavern with rough, sandstone walls. Expecting to see Littlebig locked in combat with some fearsome creature, you are not prepared for what you do see. Running to attack you are two identical dwarves, both the exact likeness of Littlebig. One of them must surely be a Doppelgänger that has turned itself into a duplicate of Littlebig and used mind control to force him to attack. But which one is the Doppelgänger and which one is the real Littlebig? You have seconds to decide before they are upon you. If you want to fight the Littlebig to your left, turn to **97**. If you want to fight the Littlebig to your right, turn to **360**.

406

You are about five metres up the rope when suddenly the bottom of it starts to curl upwards to wrap itself around your body. It is not a rope that you are holding on to but a dreaded HANGING SNAKE that is able to disguise itself cleverly. You must decide quickly what to do. If you want to drop to the floor, turn to **73**. If you would rather use your sword to hack at the snake, turn to **388**.

407

Suddenly the door closes behind you with a loud bang. You spin around to see two framed canvases hanging on the wall on either side of the door. Curiously the canvases are blank. But then you notice outline images start to appear on both of them. At the same time you feel an uncomfortable tingling sensation in your fingers and toes. The canvases soon turn into portraits, as though some invisible artist is painting them quickly. Then you recognize the people in the portraits – it is Littlebig and you! You try to run for the door but are now too weak to move. You look at Littlebig and are alarmed to see that he is no more than a shadow of his former self. You look down at your body and see that it is virtually transparent. You are both disappearing into another dimension and only your portraits will remain in this world. Your adventure is over.

CHOOSE YOUR ADVENTURER

Here at your disposal are three adventurers to choose from. Over the page are the rules for Fighting Fantasy to help you on your way. However, if you wish to begin your adventure immediately, study the characters carefully, log their attributes on the *Adventure Sheet* and you can begin!

Enzo Wolfeyes

For years the name Wolfeyes rang through Allansia, carrying with it tales of daring do, success and treasure. But a sustained run of bad luck, some poor decisions and a general lack of adventure have worn away at the reputation and slowly but surely erased it from people's minds. They have worn away too at Enzo's gold reserves and now he is in Fang, down to his last few copper pieces, just another unknown adventurer in a sea of similar figures.

Perhaps all is about to change though. Enzo has risen from penury and anonymity before. Born to a lowly peasant family in Drystone, just to the south of Darkwood Forest, Enzo escaped from home at an early age to seek his fame and fortune as an adventurer. Now he must seek it again. Fortunately for him the one thing not to have diminished recently is his strong, muscular frame and immense power. With the fire of determination burning in his breast, one day soon he knows that Wolfeyes will again be whispered in awe.

Skill	9
Stamina	24
Luck	7

Jamlo Ray

Jamlo's small stature and sleight frame have fooled many a blackguard into thinking he is an easy target as he pursues the solitary life of an adventurer, travelling alone from one place to another across often treacherous terrain, the home of thieves and murderers. How wrong they were. Those who know Jamlo well could have warned them, for despite his appearance, he is a talented swordsman and is fiercely respected for his skill and wisdom. It is a favourite saying amongst his friends that he makes light work of the most difficult situations, and brings light to the most difficult problems.

But now Jamlo needs to call on his strengths more than ever before. In a rare moment of foolhardiness, he entered Port Blacksand – better known as the City of Thieves – in the pursuit of adventure. Unfortunately, the inn he chose to lodge in was the target of a marauding bunch of pirates. Although his life was saved by a fellow adventurer who went by the name Barik Shabdark, all his possessions and, worst of all, his gold, were stolen. With only the clothes on his back and few coins in his pocket, he has found himself in Fang, desperately seeking fresh adventure.

Skill	12
Stamina	19
Luck	9

Hannabella Dehab

Hannabella is the daughter of a wealthy merchant from the prosperous town of Silverton. She could, if she wished, live comfortably in her father's home with her every whim taken care of, waiting for an eligible bachelor to come along and marry her. But that's not quite Hannabella's style – she prefers the life of the adventurer, sleeping where she lays her sword and testing herself against the most fearsome opposition she can find.

In her time, she has amassed huge wealth … although she knows only too well the dangers of getting too comfortable. Whenever she fells the lull of the quiet life back in Silverton, she gives away all her gold to worthy causes. Whether it's then natural luck or the favour of the gods pleased by such deeds, good fortune always comes her way and her treasure trove is swiftly replenished. Recently penniless yet again, Hannabella has no doubt that something good will turn up soon now that she has taken up lodgings in Fang.

Skill	8
Stamina	20
Luck	12

RULES AND EQUIPMENT

Before embarking on your adventure, you must first determine your own strengths and weaknesses.

Use dice to determine your initial SKILL, STAMINA and LUCK scores. On pages 220–221 there is an *Adventure Sheet* which you may use to record the details of an adventure. On it you will find boxes for recording your SKILL, STAMINA and LUCK scores.

You are advised to either record your scores on the *Adventure Sheet* in pencil, or make photocopies of the page to use in future adventures.

Skill, Stamina and Luck

Roll one die. Add 6 to this number and enter this total in the SKILL box on the *Adventure Sheet*.

Roll both dice. Add 12 to the number rolled and enter this total in the STAMINA box.

There is also a LUCK box. Roll one die, add 6 to this number and enter this total in the LUCK box.

For reasons that will be explained below, SKILL, STAMINA and LUCK scores change constantly during an adventure. You must keep an accurate record of these scores and for this reason you are advised either to write small in the boxes or to keep an eraser handy. But never rub out your *Initial* scores. Although you may be awarded additional SKILL, STAMINA and LUCK points, these totals may never exceed your *Initial* scores except on very rare occasions, when you will be instructed on a particular page.

Your SKILL score reflects your swordsmanship and general fighting expertise; the higher the better. Your STAMINA score reflects your general constitution, your will to survive, your determination and overall fitness; the higher your STAMINA score, the longer you will be able to survive. Your LUCK score indicates how naturally lucky a person you are. Luck – and magic – are facts of life in the fantasy kingdom you are about to explore.

Battles

You will often come across pages in the book which instruct you to fight a creature of some sort. An option to flee may be given, but if not – or if you choose to attack the creature anyway – you must resolve the battle as described below.

First record the creature's SKILL and STAMINA scores in the first vacant Monster Encounter Box on your *Adventure Sheet*. The scores for each creature are given in the book each time you have an encounter.

The sequence of combat is then:

1. Roll both dice once for the creature. Add its SKILL score. This total is the creature's Attack Strength.
2. Roll both dice once for yourself. Add the number rolled to your current SKILL score. This total is your Attack Strength.

3. If your Attack Strength is higher than that of the creature, you have wounded it. Proceed to step 4. If the creature's Attack Strength is higher than yours, it has wounded you. Proceed to step 5. If both Attack Strength totals are the same, you have avoided each other's blows – start the next Attack Round from step 1 above.

4. You have wounded the creature, so subtract 2 points from its STAMINA score. You may use your LUCK here to do additional damage (see over).

5. The creature has wounded you, so subtract 2 points from your own STAMINA score. Again, you may use LUCK at this stage (see over).

6. Make the appropriate adjustments to either the creature's or your own STAMINA scores (and your LUCK score if you used LUCK – see over).

7. Begin the next Attack Round by returning to your current SKILL score and repeating steps 1–6. This sequence continues until the STAMINA score of either you or the creature you are fighting has been reduced to zero (death).

Fighting More Than One Creature

If you come across more than one creature in a particular encounter, the instructions on that page will tell you how to handle the battle. Sometimes you will treat them as a single monster; sometimes you will fight each one in turn.

Luck

At various times during your adventure, either in battles or when you come across situations in which you could either be lucky or unlucky (details of these are given on the pages themselves), you may call on your LUCK to make the outcome more favourable. But beware! Using LUCK is a risky business, and if you are *un*lucky, the results could be disastrous.

The procedure for using your LUCK is as follows: roll two dice. If the number rolled is equal to or less than your current LUCK score, you have been lucky and the result will go in your favour. If the number rolled is higher than your current LUCK score, you have been unlucky and you will be penalized.

This procedure is known as *Testing your Luck*. Each time you *Test your Luck*, you must subtract 1 point from your current LUCK score. Thus you will soon realize that the more you rely on your LUCK, the more risky this will become.

Using Luck in Battles

On certain pages of the book you will be told to *Test your Luck* and will be told the consequences of your being lucky or unlucky. However, in battles, you always have the option of using your LUCK either to inflict a more serious wound on a creature you have just wounded, or to minimize the effects of a wound the creature has just inflicted on you.

If you have just wounded the creature, you may *Test your Luck* as described above. If you are Lucky, you have inflicted a severe wound and may subtract an extra 2 points from the creature's SKILL score. However, if you are Unlucky, the wound was a mere graze and you must restore 1 point to the creature's STAMINA (i.e. instead of scoring the normal 2 points of damage, you have now scored only 1).

If the creature has just wounded you, you may *Test your Luck* to try to minimize the wound. If you are Lucky, you have managed to avoid the full damage of the blow. Restore 1 point of STAMINA (i.e. instead of doing 2 points of damage it has done only 1). If you are Unlucky, you have taken a more serious blow. Subtract 1 extra STAMINA point.

Remember that you must subtract 1 point from your LUCK score every time you *Test your Luck.*

Restoring Skill, Stamina and Luck

Skill

Your SKILL score will not change much during your adventure. Occasionally, a page may give instructions to increase or decrease your SKILL score. A Magic Weapon may increase your SKILL, but remember that only one weapon can be used at a time! You cannot claim 2 SKILL bonuses for carrying two Magic Swords. Your SKILL score can never exceed its *Initial* value unless specifically instructed.

Stamina

Your STAMINA score will change a lot during your adventure as you fight monsters and undertake arduous tasks. As you near your goal, your STAMINA level may be dangerously low and battles may be particularly risky, so be careful!

Your backpack contains enough Provisions for ten meals. You may rest and eat at any time except when engaged in a Battle. Eating a meal restores 4 STAMINA points. When you eat a meal, add 4 points to your STAMINA.

Remember also that your STAMINA score may never exceed its *Initial* value unless specifically instructed on a page.

Luck

Additions to your LUCK score are awarded through the adventure when you have been particularly lucky. Details are given on the pages of this book. Remember that, as with SKILL and STAMINA, your LUCK score may never exceed its *Initial* value unless specifically instructed on a page.

ALTERNATIVE DICE

If you do not have a pair of dice handy, dice rolls are printed throughout the book at the bottom of the pages. Flicking rapidly through the book and stopping on a page will give you a random dice roll. If you need to 'roll' only one die, read only the first printed die; if two, total the two dice symbols.

FIGHTING FANTASY

ADVENTURE SHEET

SKILL
Initial Skill = 7

STAMINA
Initial Stamina = 7

3 3

LUCK
Initial Luck = 7

NOTES AND ITEMS

Axe head

Garlic

25 gold pieces

bronze handle dagger

Ophecic crystal

dagger

kris

knife Gold

elven stone inside
boot

MONSTER
ENCOUNTER
BOXES

SKILL =
STAMINA =

SKILL =
STAMINA =

SKILL =
STAMINA =

SKILL =
STAMINA =

SKILL =
STAMINA =

SKILL =
STAMINA =

SKILL =
STAMINA =

SKILL =
STAMINA =

SKILL =
STAMINA =

TURN OVER IF YOU DARE

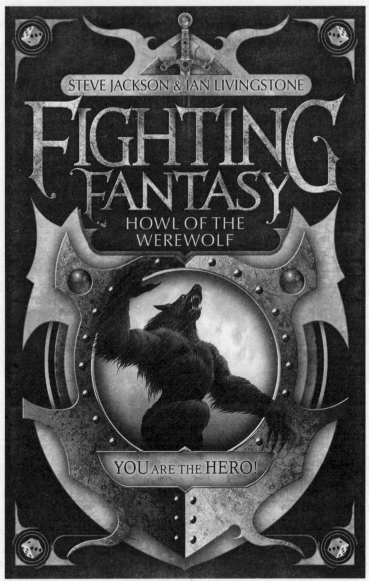

STEVE JACKSON & IAN LIVINGSTONE

FIGHTING FANTASY

HOWL OF THE WEREWOLF

YOU ARE THE HERO!

HOWL OF THE WEREWOLF

The evil land of Lupravia.
A dreadful affliction.
Can YOU overcome the powers of darkness that
are ruled by the Howl of the Werewolf?

You can hear the wolves panting as they run, easily keeping pace with you. The night is closing in, a smothering shroud of darkness. You trip over exposed tree roots, the moon – only a matter of nights away from being full – casting its sickly light through naked, black branches above. To your agitated mind the trees seem to claw at you with skeletal black fingers.

Dragging yourself up, your heart racing, your breathing shallow and fast, you spin round, scouring the oppressive forest for the tell-tale signs that you know must be there. And then you see them, a dozen blazing-red eyes, smouldering like coals, watching you from the darkness.

Growling, the wolves slink into the moonlight in front of you. Darting anxious glances around, you realise, to your horror, that you are surrounded.

And then a snarl more menacing and blood-chilling than any you have yet heard this hateful night causes the wolves halt as one. Pushing aside the other wolves as it moves through the pack is the undoubtable leader.

The creature is huge, a monstrous beast twice the size of any other wolf in the pack. Its pelt is utterly black, apart from the one long streak of grey that runs from the top of its head all the way down its back. The look of evil intent is in its eyes, something wholly unnatural in a wolf, something almost inhumanly human. A guttural growl that speaks of your imminent demise rises from deep within its chest and the wolves begin to move again. With death reflected in its eyes, the great wolf prepares to pounce.

Turn to paragraph 1.

With the wolf pack steadily closing in on you, and the great wolf tensed ready to attack in an instant, you are going to have to act fast and use all your cunning if you are ever going to get out of this dire situation alive. Will you:

Turn your back on the wolf and try to run for it? Turn to **2**

Stand your ground and prepare to meet the Black Wolf's inevitable attack? Turn to **3**

Seize the initiative and charge the wolf? Turn to **6**

2

Spinning on your heel you hurl yourself away from the leader of the pack even as the monstrous wolf springs forwards, claws bared. But are your reflexes faster than those of a deadly predator? *Test your Skill.* If you succeed, turn to **7**. If you fail, turn to **8**.

3

Feeling the familiar, reassuring weight of the blade in your hand, you take deep, measured breaths to calm yourself, and prepare to meet the beast's attack. With a snarl, the creature is on you.

BLACK WOLF   SKILL 8   STAMINA 9

After two further Attack Rounds, or if you reduce the Black Wolf's STAMINA to 7 or less, whichever comes sooner, turn at once to **9**.

4

You wake from a feverish and terrifyingly realistic dream, in which a wolf is snapping at you with slavering jaws. You open your eyes and find yourself looking up at the cobwebbed rafters of a wooden shack.

You are lying on the uncomfortable, straw-stuffed mattress of a pallet bed. You force yourself to sit up and gasp in pain from the savage wolf bite you received to your shoulder. 'You want to take care of that,' you hear a gruff voice say and you turn in surprise – wincing again as the wound smarts – to see a thickset, bearded man sitting at a table next to a stone chimney breast, smoking a pipe. His careworn face is lit by the dull orange glow of a fire, crackling in the hearth. 'I've cleaned and dressed the wound as best I can but it's going to take time to heal.' A candle burns in the window and outside all is shrouded in darkness.

Not really sure where you are, who the man is, or why he's chosen to take care of you, you mumble your thanks. 'Come, sit. There's something I have to show you.' Cautiously you rise from the bed and join the man at the table. 'I'm Ulrich, and I make my living as forester in these wild woods,' he says, proffering his hand as you take a seat. On the table in front of the woodsman is a bundle of coarse, bloodstained cloth.

Ulrich relates his version of events. He was inside his shack when he heard the wolves howling and your cries. Taking up his axe, he rushed to your aid. 'I managed to lay a savage wound on that black wolf,' he explains. 'Sent it packing, the rest of its sorry pack scurrying after, once they saw their leader bested.'

'You wanted to show me something,' you remind Ulrich.

'Indeed I do,' he mutters, and begins to unwrap the bundle in front of him. 'I told you I dealt the wolf a savage blow. Well, in fact, I cut off its paw. At least, it was a paw to begin with…' Ulrich peels back the last strip of bloodstained cloth, 'But tell me, does that look like a paw to you?'

Lying on the table in front of you is a gnarled black-furred claw, somewhere between a human hand and a wolf's paw. Horror twists your heart in its chilling grip. Before Ulrich even has a chance to explain, you already know what he is going to say. 'That wasn't a wolf that attacked you out there in the woods tonight. It was a …'

'Werewolf!' you finish. You know what this means. It would explain your feverishness and horrible hallucinatory dream. For the bite of a werewolf – a man cursed to take on the form of a wolf when moonlight bathes the world – carries the dread disease of lycanthropy, the selfsame affliction that is responsible for its own ghastly transformation. It is as good as a death sentence, for without a cure, the only future you can look forward to is one of madness and murder, as the wolf inside you struggles to free itself and satisfy its bloodlust.

You stare at the grotesque object lying on the table. Even as you watch, it appears to become more human and less animal in form. Seeing your reaction, Ulrich says, 'This is an evil thing and should be destroyed. Throw it into the fire and be done with it.'

Do you want to throw the changing hand into the fire immediately (turn to 10), or do you want to take a closer look at it first (turn to 5)?

5

Taking the hand in your own, by the flickering amber light of the fire you examine it. The hand is now almost completely human, except that it still sports particularly long and hardened claw-like nails. But there is something else. On the middle finger there is a large gold signet ring bearing a remarkable crest on its circular face. The crest shows a howling wolf's head against a full moon. You may keep this morbid curiosity if you wish. Turn to 10.

6

Drawing on all your reserves of desperate, adrenalin-fuelled courage, with your sword raised above your head, you charge the wolf even as it launches itself at you. But having seized the initiative, it is you who lands the first blow. The wolf squeals in pain, and then, its pain turned to anger, it is upon you.

BLACK WOLF   SKILL 7   STAMINA 8

After two further Attack Rounds, or if you reduce the Black Wolf's STAMINA to 7 or less, whichever happens first, turn at once to 9.

7

You throw yourself out of the way as the wolf lands hunched on the spot where you were standing only a moment before. But you are still surrounded by the rest of the pack. You abruptly find yourself face-to-face with two particularly mangy-looking, slavering specimens that try to rake you with their ragged claws while their fellows howl encouragement. Fight the wolves both at the same time.

	SKILL	STAMINA
First WOLF	7	6
Second WOLF	6	5

After you have fought two Attack Rounds against the wolves the monstrous Black Wolf – tiring of waiting for its fellows to finish you – joins the battle.

BLACK WOLF   SKILL 8   STAMINA 9

You now find yourself fighting all three wolves at the same time. After two further Attack Rounds, or if you reduce the Black Wolf's STAMINA to 7 or less, which-ever is sooner, turn at once to **9**.

8

Even as you turn to run you sense the monstrous wolf launch itself into the air behind you. There is a moment of terrible stillness and then the full weight of the creature lands on top of you, sending you sprawling on the ground. You gasp in pain, the breath knocked out of you, as the wolf sinks its cruel teeth into your shoulder and rakes your back with its steel-sharp claws. (Lose 4 STAMINA points.)

You suddenly hear a gruff voice bellowing at the beast to release you. You feel the wolf on top of you tense. The pressure of the steel gin-trap of its jaws around your shoulder abruptly eases, as your would-be killer's attention is drawn to the new arrival. The wolf gives voice to its blood-curdling growl and you feel it rumbling through your body as the weight of the beast still pins you to the cold, damp floor of the forest.

There is another shout and then an agonised yelping. The weight on top of you is released. Hearing another howl of pain you manage to roll onto your side. But something is wrong; you feel woozy and your head starts to spin. Your vision greying, you see a tall, thickset figure standing over the Black Wolf, a sturdy woodsman's axe in his hand. The axe descends again and the wolf gives a strangled yowl. The axeman swings his makeshift weapon again, landing another blow, and the wolf flees yelping, the rest of the pack skulking after their leader. Then the hulking figure is looming over you. Overcome by pain and blood loss, your body cannot take any more and you black out. Turn to 4.

<h2 style="text-align:center">9</h2>

As you battle the Black Wolf you become increasingly aware of the rest of the wolf pack continuing to close in around you, and that momentary distraction is all it takes. You stumble on an exposed root and lose your footing. The huge wolf seizes the opportunity with unnerving animal cunning. Your sword-arm flailing as you try to maintain your balance, the wolf smashes through your compromised defence and hurls you bodily to the ground. You feel its great weight on top of you, the breath knocked out of you. You can smell its foetid, carnivore's breath, hear its snarl in your ear. And then, with a savage cry of animal satisfaction, the wolf sinks its fangs into the flesh of your shoulder. (Lose 2 STAMINA points.) Your agonised cry is suddenly joined by a howl of pain as the wolf releases its grip. Your vision greying, you see a tall, thickset figure standing over the Black Wolf, a sturdy woodsman's axe raised above his head. The axe descends again and the wolf gives a strangled yowl and leaps off you. The woodsman swings his axe again and the wolf flees yelping, the rest of the pack skulking after their leader. Then the great figure is looming over you. Defeated by pain and blood loss, your body cannot take any more and you black out. Turn to 4.

Picking up the transformed hand you hurl it into the fire with a scream of rage and then watch as the fingers blacken and burn, the flesh crisping and crackling in the hungry flames.

'Then I am doomed,' you say, in utter despair as you gaze into the fire. 'Doomed to become a creature of bloodthirsty appetites I shall be unable to control when the moon waxes full. I shall be an outcast, an animal, a murderous beast.'

'Maybe not,' Ulrich says, fixing you with an unnerving stare. There is something old and forbidding about the dark pits of his eyes, as if there is something else looking out of Ulrich at you. 'There may still be hope – for you.'

There is? Then what is to be done? You press the woodsman to tell you more. What does he know that you do not?

'I know of two cures for lycanthropy, but we will have to act quickly.' Ulrich will help you? But why? 'Let us just say that we all have our secrets.' So what are the cures? 'The surest way, is to find the werewolf that infected you with its bite, and kill it. You could also eat a sprig of the herb belladonna, if you could find some. And there is one other course of action we could take. We could seek the assistance of Grandmother Zekova, the wisest person I know, who lives further into these woods, over the border in Lupravia. But it is up to you. What do you want to do?'

To choose your next move, you must read the full version of **Howl of the Werewolf.** *Only by delving deep into the accursed land of Lupravia can you hope to overcome the dreaded shadow of lycanthropy that has descended over you. But the way will not be easy and you must act fast for the next full moon is nearly upon you and you must be cured by then – unless you are to spend the rest of your tormented days bound to the dreadful sound that is the* **Howl of the Werewolf.**

ONLINE

Stay in touch with the Fighting Fantasy community at www.fightingfantasy.com. Sign up today and receive exclusive access to:

- Fresh Adventure Sheets
- Members' forum
- Competitions
- Quizzes and polls
- Exclusive Fighting Fantasy news and updates

You can also send in your own Fighting Fantasy material, the very best of which will make it onto the website.

www.fightingfantasy.com

The website where YOU ARE THE HERO!